FATHER ABRAHAM HAS MANY SONS AND DAUGHTERS

The Family of Transformed Relationships

RABIH SABRA

WESTBOW
PRESS®
A DIVISION OF THOMAS NELSON
& ZONDERVAN

WestBow Press books may be ordered through booksellers or by contacting:

WestBow Press
A Division of Thomas Nelson & Zondervan
1663 Liberty Drive
Bloomington, IN 47403
www.westbowpress.com
844-714-3454

ISBN: 978-1-6642-2608-1 (sc)
ISBN: 978-1-6642-2609-8 (hc)
ISBN: 978-1-6642-2607-4 (e)

Library of Congress Control Number: 2021904484

Print information available on the last page.

WestBow Press rev. date: 03/19/2021

CONTENTS

FIGURES

INTRODUCTION

CAN ANYTHING GOOD COME
OUT OF THE MIDDLE EAST?

Something new is sprouting in the land that gave us Osama Bin Laden, 9/11, Al Qaeda, and ISIS. Despite its history, God is calling forth a blessing from the Middle East to the whole world—including you. The story I am about to tell you will impact your life personally and directly. From a small beginning, a seemingly insignificant community is being transformed by the gospel of Jesus Christ. Its people are modeling a different perspective of life with Jesus, one that can benefit the Church worldwide. I call it a Transforming Community because it transforms both those who are in it and the surrounding community. Beginning in 1997, this transforming community, which we call the Access Team, established the first church in the thousand-year history of the Druze, as well as a technical school and a K–12 school. These groups are in turn transforming their communities through the gospel of Jesus Christ.

The Access Team blazed a new path of outreach to the Druze, and many other laborers followed. Starting with only a handful of believers among the Druze in 1997, they have grown to over two thousand in 2010. The growth came from the labor of multiple agencies that noted the new openness among the Druze and sent workers to the area, and they are still bearing a lot of fruit.

The Access Team is a group of believers in Jesus Christ connected by a particular type of relationship. It is the result of a hybrid expression of Middle Eastern and Western cultures, finding their place in the mission of God. I believe it is especially relevant in our times, providing churches worldwide with a blueprint for spiritual growth and outreach into their communities. It does not require a big budget or elaborate facilities. Best of all, you don't have to be a gifted teacher or leader to be a team member or bear bountiful eternal fruit. This type of group offers a unique and fulfilling role for every one of its members.

Technological advances in travel and communications have increased intermingling between cultures, rapidly changing our world and, in turn, changing us. We now need cross-cultural skills to connect with our next-door neighbors. The Sunday-service church model does not meet all believers' needs, and it feels like something is missing from our walk with God. We desperately need a fresh way to live within our local church. The Transforming Community team is a viable option for every church to consider, especially in cross-cultural settings and communities distant from the Christian tradition.

This book is about the type of relationships that form a Transforming Community team. It has a dual focus on transformation and relationship. It begins with an exploration of the community's biblical roots, its mission, and what it means to be the household of God. Then it will show why we need transformation, what it is, and how it happens.

Finally, by combining transformation and relationships, the book will show how Transforming Community functions. Once you've read this book, I encourage you to use an online resources on our website www.transformingcommunity.com. There you will find a step-by-step guide for individuals and teams who want to become a Transforming Community. We have also created an app named Into His Presence as a direct application of Chapter Eight. It is a tool that helps the believer to pray and meditate on the names, attributes, and essence of God.

The Access Team has its roots in Abraham's family, but I became part of it in the mid-1980s. Ted Fletcher, the founder of Pioneers (a prominent mission agency based in Florida, USA), visited us in Lebanon, where our part of the story had taken us. He made a prophetic comment about the Access Team, quoting the prophet Zechariah of the Old Testament: "Do not despise a small beginning!"

Born in Eastern culture and educated and trained in the West, I believe I have a vantage point that allows me to be both analytical and relational in my thinking. I have noticed a clear difference between the two cultures, most prominently in the area of individualism versus communalism. The people within these two cultures interact and make decisions in different ways. My goal is not to compare the two or prove which is better, but to combine them to present a better view. We don't have to be constrained to one culture; we can adapt and learn to find what is useful across cultures and apply them appropriately.

My goal in this book is to show you this model and highlight a path of transformation through the gospel of Jesus Christ. Its main message is that you cannot walk with Jesus alone; you need a family. My prayer is that this book will help you gain a new perspective on the Church and find your specific role in it, inspiring you to join or start a team of people engaged in transforming relationships.

CHAPTER ONE
TRANSFORMING ME

I got an F in physics! It was the fall of my senior year at Syracuse University. In the last week of the semester, I checked the physics class syllabus, and I thought it said the exam was on Wednesday. I went to take the exam that day, only to find the room empty; no one was there. I went to the professor's office, and he was very unsympathetic. He said, "Sorry, bud, you didn't show up for the final exam on Tuesday; you got an F." I was devastated. I left the professor's office and walked back to my apartment. The route took me down Euclid Ave, then I turned left on Westcott Ave.

Two weeks earlier, someone was handing out Bibles at that intersection, and I had taken one from him as I walked by. I had never seen a Bible before because I am a Druze from Lebanon. My people do not believe in the Bible, Jesus Christ, or Christianity. Christians were our enemies during the civil war in Lebanon, and I spent several nights of horror in my village, Qarnayel, under constant shelling coming in from the mountains to the north.

That was in 1975 when I was fifteen years old, and all my siblings had already left Lebanon; my two sisters were married, and my brother went to SUNY at Buffalo.[1] My father had passed away in 1964, so it was just my mother and I remaining. When the shelling started, we slept in the hallway because it was shielded from the outside by many walls.

---

[1] State University of New York at Buffalo.

One day, after a long night of terror and bombing, my mother decided it was time for us to leave the village. Our neighbor wanted to come along, so I had to load our car with essentials. Our neighbor had an interesting definition of essentials; I ran up and down the stairs to her house, carrying a tank of olive oil and bags of rice, beans, clothes, and other things. But she also had many silver platters, bowls, candlesticks, and other precious items. When I was coming out of her house with the olive oil, bombshells started raining down all around me. I could hear them coming in like trains thundering through the sky, a roar I can still remember. When I was opening the trunk of the car, I heard one coming in, so I put down the olive oil and dived with my face to the ground, hands on my ears, just as I had learned in our family military camp. The shell hit about two hundred feet from where I was standing, and it shook the ground. I still remember seeing little pebbles popping up off the ground as I lay flat. When I stood up, I found a four-inch hole in the car's trunk, made by flying shrapnel from the shell. If I had been standing, that hole would have been in my back.

We finally managed to get all of our things in the car and were ready to leave. None of the others with me knew how to drive, so I had to get behind the wheel of our silver stick-shift 1974 Peugeot 504; that was the first time I ever went on public roads.

These memories came back to me as I took the Bible from the evangelist at the corner of Euclid and Westcott. I was thinking, *this is the book of the Christians. They lobbed 155mm Howitzer shells at me, and now they are giving me this?* It had a picture of a man with a keffiyeh, the Middle East's emblematic scarf, on the cover, so I thought it must have had something to say about us. *So strange,* I thought, *but I guess I can look at what it says.* I took the book home with me and placed it on my desk. Old memories of my hometown and family continued to swirl in my head. Losing my father when I was four years old scarred me for life.

All I remember from that day is a long wooden box in the middle of our living room and many people coming and going. My mother was crying. I asked her what was in the box, and she replied, "Just some soil and grass." Thinking back at her answer, I suppose there was a trace of truth in it, however abstract. In the following months and years, whenever I asked where my father was, she'd say he was traveling overseas. I didn't know that box had been my father's coffin, but I connected the dots later when I was eight years old. One day, I was extremely angry with my older brother, who had been somehow messing with me. I threatened to tell our dad when he came back from travel. My brother laughed and replied, "He's not coming back; he's dead." I didn't believe him at first, but my mother confirmed it when I asked her. I can still feel the pain of not only losing my father but feeling that I had no one to run to, given that my family had kept me in the dark for four years. They were trying to protect me, but the actual effect it had made me feel insecure and wonder what other secrets were lurking out there. Who could I trust? Who was my defender?

We had two homes in Lebanon, one in Beirut and one in Qarnayel, our hometown. We spent school months in Beirut because it was too cold in the mountains that time of year. Qarnayel is perched beautifully on top of three peaks, and the name itself means "God's peak" (*Qarn* means horn or peak, and *El* means God in Hebrew). When the civil war started in 1975, we thought it would be safer to stay in Qarnayel in winter that year. The bus ride to my school in Choueifat took over an hour. We missed many school days because of scattered fighting along the bus route. One day, our bus got caught in a crossfire of machine guns. No one on the bus was hurt, but when I told my mother about what happened, she decided it was time to leave Lebanon. Leaving my home was another significant loss I suffered. Oh, how I loved our house and our orchard in Qarnayel! I enjoyed watering the cherry trees and spending the whole day with my sheep in the orchard. Those were special times of joy for me. But we had to leave them behind. The year was 1976. My father had lived in the United States for many years before he was married, and his US citizenship had transferred to us as his family, so it was natural for us to relocate there.

From the time I left Lebanon to the day I took the Bible at the street corner in 1983, I had moved eight times. I no longer formed bonds with places or people because they were always changing. My family and my home in Qarnayel no longer defined my identity; while my heart tried to cling to them, it was useless. They had nothing of substance to offer. I would eventually return to live in Qarnayel with my wife and children, discovering then that I was not alone in losing family and heritage. My whole extended family, which numbered about seven thousand, went through the same thing. We had once enjoyed a place of influence as a prominent Druze family; one of our members had been in the parliament for decades, serving as Minister of Interior and other important governmental positions. But our prominence in Lebanon vanished in the years of chaos and civil war. Even our heritage was lost as the older generation passed away one after the other, replaced by a war generation whose main concern was survival at any cost. As I grew older, I realized that our heritage was not as upright as the older generation made it out to be. Our people had their problems, too, especially with greed over inheritance and status.

There was a third sense of significant loss in my life shared by all Arabic speaking people of the Middle East. The 1967 and 1973 wars with Israel were severe blows to Arab pride and identity. A collective depression in Arab hearts and minds that spawned hatred and outbursts of anger toward Israel dominated in the ensuing decades. In Lebanon, there was a persistent public lament over the fallen glory of Palestine and the Arab identity of Jerusalem, memorialized in a famous song by Fairuz, which I must have heard a thousand times.

For you, city of prayer, I pray.

For you, city that shines in beautiful dwellings, Flower of Cities, O Jerusalem, O Jerusalem, City of prayer, for you I pray.[2]

Every time I hear that song, I get a sense of despair. The song expressed how Arabs felt about the 1967 war.

The PLO[3] had offices in Beirut, which it used to cultivate public opinion against Israel. On one occasion, a relative invited me to a movie that turned out to be a story about the Fidai'iyeen[4] fighting the Israeli occupation of Palestine. It was a heart-wrenching drama of love, hate, war, and suffering. At the time, a political movement of socialism was brewing in Lebanon, and this film conveyed a message sympathetic to that movement. When I told my mother about it, she warned me not to accept everything I heard and investigate things further. She said that my

---

[2] "Zahrat El Madaen" (Flower of Cities), first stanza.
[3] PLO stands for Palestine Liberation Organization.
[4] Means martyrs in Arabic.

father had expressed to her that he didn't like socialism. Her warning was enough for me to keep a safe distance from ideologies on either side of the conflict; nevertheless, my spirit was wounded, along with everyone else, by the grievous losses we had suffered.

The first year of civil war in Lebanon confirmed my cautious attitude toward the PLO when they effectively took control of West Beirut; our winter home lay within this territory.

On one occasion, an announcement declared an end to the civil war. The warring factions had signed a peace agreement. That turned out to be a very short-lived peace, but at the time it was announced, people went out to their balconies and started shooting their AK-47s in the air in celebration. I saw this as an opportunity to test the AK-47 my extended family had given me when I went through our youth military training camp in Qarnayel. So, despite my mother's pleas, I whipped out my machine gun and fired off a few volleys in the air. Minutes later, a PLO officer barged into our home and arrested me. I wished I had my father there to defend me against this stranger breaking into our home. If I had to get arrested for breaking the law, I wanted it to be at the Lebanese authorities' hands, not a foreigner. He dragged me to the local PLO office, where I spent several hours sweating in agony, awaiting the consequence. As it turned out, my mother made several phone calls to relatives in the Lebanese police and army, and they secured my release within a few hours. The PLO officer returned my AK-47 and gave me two extra magazines filled with bullets, but that did nothing to change my negative view of the PLO. I was so glad when they left Lebanon.

At Syracuse University, I had many Jewish friends who wanted to talk about Israel and the Arabs, and they questioned my understanding regarding the history of the region. They also reopened old wounds of enmity and hatred, and there was plenty on both sides. They, too, inherited a "wounded" culture rife with just as much hate as the Palestinians I knew in Lebanon. It became clear that both cultures were caught in a poisonous cycle; I had no wish to participate, but being from Lebanon, I represented the Arab position in the conversation by default.

The cycle of violence and hatred created deeply dysfunctional cultures on both sides, a fact that underscored in my mind just how broken the world is and how difficult it is to make any real change. War, chaos, and losses were not only part of my personal experience, but that of all Middle Eastern cultures, both Arab and Jewish; we all inherited a very nasty problem. Any real resolution in this centuries-old conflict will have to contain more than mere ideas; it has to redeem the losses suffered by both parties. Such redemptive change is not achieved by force but has to be a choice made by both parties. It is also not enough to accomplish this restoration personally; it has to spread to both communities. I often wondered what I could do to bring about such healing, which piqued my interest in community-level behavior and decision making.

On the day I got an F in physics, I went back to my apartment, where the Bible lay on my desk. There I cried in pain; I had a deep sense of loss. The failing grade unlocked a backlog of pain in my heart accumulated through many devastating losses over the years. I cried out to God and asked Him, "Why did this happen? Am I condemned to a life of losses? Why are You doing this to me?" With an academic setback, no place to call home, and a cultural heritage mired in hatred, greed, and war, I was thoroughly aware of my brokenness. I wanted to know why God had given me this life even if I couldn't do anything about it—I wanted to see the reason why I had to inherit this life of losses.

In retrospect, I think this was the moment I had to face depravity[5]— my own, and that of the world. My eyes turned to the book on the desk. I grabbed it and opened it to the Gospel of John, the first chapter: "In the beginning was the Word, and the Word was with God, and the Word was God." God was speaking, revealing Himself to me. My heart melted. I had a big fat F written in the middle of my chest: F for failure in Physics; F for losing my father at four years old and growing up without someone to defend me when I needed him; F for belonging to a culture that has been on the losing end for the past 1,000 years; and F for a homeland devoured by civil war, my home in Beirut destroyed, my home in Qarnayel occupied by strangers, my orchard left desolate. Amid my defeat, God was speaking to me.

He was in the beginning, which means that when time began, He was already there! He must have known why my life was so broken. So I pressed on and read more, finding out that what I was suffering from is everyone's

---

[5] Some synonyms to the word depravity are corruption, evil, and decadence.

condition, not just mine; we are all suffering from a case of depravity. As I read on in the Gospel of John, I came to chapter 3, in which Jesus has a conversation with Nicodemus and speaks of two worlds, one physical and another spiritual. The two discoveries I had made so far, of depravity and the existence of the two worlds, gave me hope in understanding and perhaps even solving my problem. Instead of trying to find my home within a physical world that seemed so broken and beyond repair, I could look to the spiritual realm.

I came to Jesus with a great deal of excitement, and I was ready for the perfect life, one filled with love, joy, peace, patience, and every good thing the Lord has to offer. I came to my heavenly Father so he could fix everything wrong and restore the losses in my life. At the time, I was not aware of eternal life, judgment, or salvation. I came to Him not so much to secure my future but to redeem my past. I needed rescue from depravity.

Some days after I came to Christ, a new acquaintance asked me some questions about my background. I told him my story and said, "I don't have a father; he died when I was four years old." Later that day, when I was alone, I sensed the spirit of God asking me a question: "Rabih, do you have a father?" I answered, "No, I don't." He said, "Yes, you do. I am your heavenly Father. Never say that you are fatherless." I embraced my heavenly Father, and I felt secure. My love and loyalty to Him became rock-solid almost instantly, and my losses were now transforming into gain. I was transitioning out of defeat and into victory.

Right away, I started telling everyone around me that I had found the Truth, and His name was Jesus. At the time, that was the best I could do as a witness. I told my mother and brother on the phone about my newfound faith, and they said, "It's just a phase you are going through. You have been away from your family for too long, and you are making a psychological adjustment. It's called 'transference,' and you'll transfer again to something else soon." But I knew better; God was speaking to me.

God spoke to me in His Word, the Bible. In it, I read stories of people in past generations who trusted in Him and whom God transformed into super-heroes of the faith. Hebrews 11 is a tremendous big-picture view of history and God's dealings with humanity, telling us all of their great acts were done by faith. Abraham's life attracted me mainly because he fit the profile of the patriarch of my earthly family in Qarnayel, and his family reminded me of mine. I was also somewhat familiar with the landscapes through which he traveled—from Haran through Aleppo and Damascus to Aram—so I could visualize the Genesis accounts and associate them with experiences in my own life. Another reason that Abraham's family attracted me is that I saw loss and redemption, defeat, and victory in their story. As I analyze the personal losses I suffered, I find that each falls under one of three headings: loss of protection, loss of community, and loss of my heritage. I saw all these in Abraham's household. He was moving from one place to another, struggling to survive and protect his family, and waiting for a blessing that defies human reasoning.

Abraham's life and his family do not merely parallel my own. They are the root cause of my losses—and, as it turned out, my victories as well. I wasn't suffering defeat because of accidental circumstances or intellectual and psychological strategies; rather, I was reaping the harvest of historically documented events that even now continue to unfold in my life and the lives of everyone around me.

CHAPTER TWO
TRANSFORMATION IN THE HOUSEHOLD OF GOD

The Bible is a love story. John 3:16 summarizes the story well: "For God so loved the world that he gave his one and only son that whoever believes in him shall not perish but have eternal life." It begins in eternity past, before creation. The Father and the Son together initiated their plan for redemption through the blood of Jesus Christ.[6] The story has included generations of people from all cultures and backgrounds, and it continues today. It is not complete until all the children of God have made their contribution and written the story of their lives in it.[7]

I say it is a love story because it reveals the great love that God has for us and teaches us what love is, showing that God is love. He demonstrates His love through His active creation, by which He made the universe, fine-tuned it to sustain life, and gave humans awareness and understanding so that we could relate to Him.

There are several climaxes and peaks in the love story, which began even before creation when the Father and the Son entered into a covenant to redeem creation. What prophetic mystery it holds! At the center of the whole story, we find one towering peak: the Cross. The death, burial, and

---

[6] The Eternal Covenant, Hebrews 13:20
[7] Andrew F. Walls, "The Ephesian Moment," The Cross-Cultural Process in Christian History (Maryknoll, New York: Orbis Books, 2002), pp. 72–81.

resurrection of Jesus Christ brought resolution of all conflicts in Abraham's household. It redeemed all losses suffered and conferred all the blessings promised. It paid for all the sins of the family and those of the whole world.[8]

The story tells us that God desires a relationship with us and wants us to belong to Him. He sent his one and only Son to die on our behalf; this is the ultimate revelation of His love, through which He redeems us, pays for our sins, and brings us into His family.

FATHER ABRAHAM HAS MANY SONS AND DAUGHTERS

I am part of God's great love story, authored and set in motion in space and time by God Himself; I am a thread in it. The story is well beyond my comprehension, so I could never figure it out on my own, but only as He reveals it to me in His Word and by the Holy Spirit.

The Bible is the story of God's dealings with His creation, told through prophets and apostles who were inspired to write—it is a joint effort between God and man. The Bible is God's revelation to all who can see and hear, and I accept it as the highest authority on the person and character of God and all else that flows from that understanding.

The story of Abraham's family is still developing today; his friendship with God has become the foundation of both the Old and New Covenants. His family's loyalties and conflicts have shaped the destiny of nations. The relationship between Ishmael and Isaac is at the root of the Arab-Israeli conflict we are still living in today. Out of the same family, war and peace, hatred and love, and curses and blessings have rippled throughout the world for thousands of years.

The story of Abraham and his family tells us that *God is revealing His righteousness to all creation by transforming His household into the likeness of His Son, Jesus Christ.* He promised Abraham and his descendants a blessing,[9] which they tried to apprehend in their strength. But they

---

[8] 1 John 2:2.

[9] Genesis 12:1–3, 15:18, and 22:16–18.

consistently failed and finally had to let go of it, and only then did God grant it to them as a gift.

THE BLESSING

God called Abraham to leave his father's house in Ur, which is northern Iraq today. He didn't tell Abraham where to go, just to leave, and Abraham had to trust that God would show him later where to go. Abraham obeyed God by faith.[10] As the years went by, God and Abraham built a relationship, and Abraham became known as the friend of God. God was pleased with Abraham and promised him that He would make him the father of many nations and that his descendants would be God's people. God repeats this promise four times in the Genesis account (chapters 12, 15, 17, and 22). In chapter 22, after Abraham willingly offers Isaac in obedience to God's command, God doubles the blessing. The New Living Translation says, "Certainly, I will bless you." Other translations read, "In blessing, I will bless you"[11] and "Indeed, I will bless you."[12]

Not only does God double the blessing, but He also swears by His Name. The words of emphasis are unique to chapter 22; they are not in the first three accounts. I believe this is because God got emotional, moved by Abraham's obedience on Mount Moriah; there, at God's command, Abraham willingly laid down what he had waited for most of his life. There is no record that he asked Sarah's opinion before he took Isaac to offer him as a sacrifice; he just obeyed and went. Abraham didn't know how the situation would resolve either, only that God was in control and would find a way to make it work out for good. He trusted God. This act of faith is what moved God to restate His promises to Abraham, this time with double emphasis and sealed by His Name. The most profound guarantee of the promises made to Abraham is that God wanted to make them happen, and what God wants, He does. God is not only bound by His word but by His desire as well.

Members of Abraham's household recounted the promises and often spoke of the friendship between God and Abraham. They were all

---

[10] Hebrews 11:8–22.

[11] NKJV

[12] NASB

mobilized on several occasions when the angel of the Lord came to visit; upon each visit, Abraham would ask his household to prepare a calf and bread for his Friend, a meal that takes all day to cook. They referred to their relationship with God and His presence among them with the phrase "the Blessing,"[13] and new generations in the household learned of it early in life. They competed for it and, at times, flaunted it.[14] The Blessing was central in Abraham's house; it was the most precious thing they had, and it set them apart from every other family anywhere in the world.

The Blessing also caused problems in the family. Starting with Abraham and Sarah, they tried to fulfill the promise by their own means. Abraham took Hagar, Sarah's maid, and she conceived a son for him. Ishmael grew up to become the father of the Arab nations, whom God has blessed with great favor and wealth.[15] Although Abraham rejoiced over Ishmael, he was not to be the fulfillment of the promise of God. God waited until Sarah was ninety years old, and then He fulfilled His promise, allowing her to become pregnant with Isaac. There is a pattern here; nothing Abraham and Sarah did in their strength resulted in any success, whereas everything that God did led them closer to the Blessing.

Then God asked Abraham to lay down the blessing again, this time on the altar on Mount Moriah. Abraham willingly laid down Isaac, whom he considered to be the Blessing. But in laying him down, Abraham found the Blessing in the sacrificial lamb, a sign that foretold the coming of the Messiah.

Every generation since then had to undergo the same test, but only a handful found the Blessing. They found it when they realized God Himself is the Blessing, not the land, not the descendants who would become nations, not the heritage, ritual, or whatever else they thought the promise contained. They had to consciously and deliberately trade the land inheritance for God.

It wasn't easy to pass down the Blessing; it was not as simple as the father laying hands on his son and pronouncing a blessing upon him. Even before they came out of the womb, the twins Esau and Jacob competed

---

[13] Genesis 25:11; 28:4; 46:3; 49:8–12; Matthew 1:1–16.

[14] Genesis 37:1–10.

[15] Genesis 21:17–18.

for it. The blessing God gave to Abraham passed to Isaac, so they assumed it would have to go to one of the twins, and the firstborn was in line to get it. The name Jacob means "the one that follows next." It also means "deceiver or crooked." Neither meaning is a compliment, so why in the world would parents give their son such a name? Being named Mr. Second Place or Mr. Crooked is not a good thing, and it became Jacob's purpose in life to change his destiny and come in first. He wanted most to get the Blessing; he sought it with all his wits and resources. One day, Esau came back from the field very hungry, and Jacob used the opportunity to buy his birthright with a bowl of lentil soup. Jacob thought that would bring him a step closer to getting the Blessing. Rebekah, the mother of the twins, wove a plot of deception to take the blessing from Esau, the first-born, and give it to Jacob. When Isaac was in a ripe old age, he called Esau to his tent and asked him to go out and hunt a gazelle, to cook it and bring it to him, and then he would give him the blessing. Rebekah heard what Isaac told Esau, so she quickly called Jacob and told him to kill a sheep and prepare it and bring it to his father, who was nearly blind. Jacob tricked his father Isaac into blessing him instead of Esau. He stole his father's blessing.

Esau married outside the family, but Jacob was careful to marry his cousins because he wanted to please his father and maintain his claim to the blessing. In dealing with his uncle Laban and Laban's shepherds, Jacob worked hard to protect his own best interests and gain the upper hand in every transaction. Doing business with Jacob was not a win for both parties; many people who did business with him ended up losing. Jacob gathered considerable wealth through his schemes, but he eventually had to give it all up. After many years of living and working with his uncle Laban, Jacob found he was no longer welcome in Laban's household, having made too much money from him. As Jacob traveled back home, he heard that his brother Esau was coming out to meet him with four hundred men. Jacob thought for sure Esau was coming for his life after the trick he pulled many years ago, stealing the blessing. That night he sent out his herds and shepherds ahead of him to meet his brother Esau in an attempt to absorb the shock of anger Esau would surely feel. After the flocks, Jacob sent Leah and her children, keeping Rachel last because he loved her the most. Eventually, he released even her to protect the dearest thing he had—himself. At that point, Jacob had lost all his protection and family and still hadn't obtained the Blessing. When he was alone at night, he wrestled with God till morning and finally prevailed when he put Him in a lock. Jacob would not release the angel of God until the angel blessed him. So the angel of the Lord dislocated Jacob's hip, changed his name from Jacob to Israel, and blessed him according to his petition. For Jacob to finally receive the Blessing, he had to apprehend God.

A fundamental question arises from this passage: If Jacob already had the blessing through his father, why did he insist that the angel of the Lord bless him? Jacob knew there was something more; he came to realize that the real Blessing is God Himself.

God's Blessing was more than an offer of friendship; God's justice and mercy had to be satisfied at once to grant Jacob's request. Only when Jacob let go of all he considered precious, including his own life, did he find God. When he let go of the earthly blessing, he saw God, who became his protection, family, and the Blessing he sought. He named the place where he wrestled with God *Penuel* because he saw God's face and lived. Here the Blessing is spelled out for us in plain language: to come into God's presence and live.

When God gave Moses the Law and commandments, they were all centered on coming into the presence of God. God's people had to go through extensive labor each day and satisfy every minute detail just to secure a few moments in the presence of God for one representative priest, once a year. If they ignored any aspect of the ritual, fire came out of the Holy of Holies and consumed the priest.[16] Yet some, like Jacob, found a way to go into God's presence without ritual and survive. The road was available to them even in the days of the patriarchs and the Law.[17]

God indeed is the Blessing promised to Abraham and all his spiritual descendants. God pledged Himself to Abraham! He alone makes land flow with milk and honey; only He gives peace and makes it possible for the hungry to be satisfied[18] no matter how much food they have. It is not biblical to regard the land alone, without God, as the promise given to Abraham. Still, Arabs and Jews have been fighting over it for centuries,

---

[16] Leviticus 10.
[17] Hebrews 7.
[18] Hosea 4:10 and Micah 6:14.

disregarding God's desire for mercy and justice and trying to lay hold of the promise with their strength. God promised Himself to Abraham first and foremost, and only through fellowship with God would the blessing of land be delivered. The blessing He promised is not attainable through personal effort but only through yielding ourselves to Him. Throughout the history of the nation of Israel, God teaches us that we must worship God on His terms, not ours.

In my encounter with God, He laid hold of me and thus became my protector, my family, and my blessing. He replaced the counterfeits I had before with what is real and eternal. Biblical truth released me from the yoke of bondage and enmity against Israel, and I believe that it can release every Arab and Jew as well. The good news of the New Testament is that Jesus Christ has destroyed this hostility between the children of Abraham and made it possible for all people of all ethnic backgrounds to be part of Abraham's family and partakers of the promise by adoption. The coming of Jesus does not nullify the land promises made to Abraham and his descendants, but He will not fulfill these promises while Israel is in rebellion. They will be fulfilled by God when they believe in Jesus, the Messiah.

The lives of the patriarchs demonstrate clearly that God's promises are not attainable apart from God, whether in the Old or the New Testament times. Today, some Bible teachers deny the people of Israel their promise by asserting its validity yet ignoring the essential truth that they must come to Jesus Christ to get the Blessing. The land promises cannot be fulfilled apart from Him, for there is no salvation or fulfillment of God's promises apart from Jesus Christ.[19] Relationship with God transformed Jacob from Mr. Second-Place Deceiver to the one who entered God's presence and lived.

The disciples of Jesus experienced a similar transformation. Before they met Jesus, they were poor, uneducated fishermen trying to survive under their cruel Roman oppressors. Being physical descendants of Abraham, they were waiting for the Messiah, and as they came to know Jesus better, they realized that it was He. Now, the disciples entered their relationship with Jesus with a long list of expectations of what the Messiah's role would

---

[19] 2 Corinthians 1:20.

be, a list that was handed down to them through generations of religious tradition. As Messiah, He should deliver Israel from the Romans and elevate the Jews over the Gentile nations.[20] He was to honor tradition, disregard women, and stay away from Gentiles. They wanted Jesus to pay the temple tax, to hobnob with the religious establishment, to be crowned King of the Jews, and to give them seats of power among their people. They encouraged Him to call down legions of warriors from heaven to His defense and to evade death on the cross. Jesus fulfilled none of these wishes. Instead, on the last night before His crucifixion, in the upper room where they met, He wrapped a towel around His waist and washed their feet.

He then told them, "Since I, your Lord and Teacher, have washed your feet, you ought to wash each other's feet."[21] Before Jesus was crucified and rose from the dead, they were arguing about who was the greatest among them.[22] At the Last Supper, their dreams of grandeur, of sitting on thrones next to Jesus, were gone; instead, Jesus instructed them to become foot washers.

They had to lay down what they thought was the Blessing for the sake of following Jesus. They could not maintain a belief in Jesus as the Messiah and at the same time keep their traditions; it was either/or, not both.

Fast forward a couple of months: shortly after the day of Pentecost, we read in Acts 3 that Peter and John went up to the temple to pray. At the gate, they saw a lame beggar who was born paralyzed. Looking eye to eye, Peter said to the man, "I don't have any silver or gold for you. But I'll give you what I have. In the name of Jesus Christ, the Nazarene, get up and walk!" What a fantastic transformation in Peter; he knew He had power from above to speak forth miracles on earth, and he faithfully did so. After the Holy Spirit indwelt the disciples, their lives were radically transformed, and they willingly laid down their lives for Jesus Christ. This transformation is the hallmark of being connected to Jesus Christ, and it involves first letting go of something in preparation for receiving something else.[23]

---

[20] Acts 1:6.
[21] John 13:14.
[22] Matthew 18:1–4; Mark 9:33–36; Luke 9:46–47.
[23] Matthew 13:44.

As I continue to study the Word of God, I gain confidence that what I experienced when I read the Gospel of John for the first time was real. I knew that what my mother described as "just a phase" was how God had been dealing with humanity since the beginning of history. The transformation I was experiencing was not just a psychological adjustment I made to compensate for my losses.

It was something God was doing in me; I was becoming a new creation of His as He poured Himself into me and put me on display as a witness to His righteousness. I was in good company with the remnant—the patriarchs, prophets, and apostles of Hebrews 11—since we had this transformation experience in common. I began to see my life as a continuation of their story; I am connected to them by faith and history, telling of God's righteousness.

FROM REVELATION TO RELATIONSHIP

The Bible tells the love story in many passages; it is a consistent theme throughout the Bible, from Genesis to Revelation. In the love story between God and humankind, there are many threads, two of which are revelation and relationship; both reflect God's character. The essence of love is a yearning to know and to be known by another. Revelation is at the core of love. It is the radiance of God, who wants to be known by the creation He loves, and He wants His creation to respond in worship.

The New Testament reveals the Trinity of God as a household.[24] The Father is the Head, and He gave the Son authority, sent Him into the world, and told Him what to say. In turn, the Son gives glory to the Father and submits to His will. Both the Father and the Son sent the Holy Spirit, whose mission is to reveal the Son.[25] The gospel's unfathomable miracle is that God has joined us to The Trinity's holy community, making us members of His household.

Revealed in a family of Father, Son, Holy Spirit, and Church, God's

---

[24] Bishop Leslie Newbigin's series of lectures on the household of God is a valuable resource for understanding this concept. See www.logos.com/product/121478/the-household-of-god-lectures- on-the-nature-of-church.

[25] John 14:1; John 17; Hebrews 1. The Father, Son, and Holy Spirit are equally God, yet within the Trinity, there are clear distinctions in position and role (Ryrie 1986).

love operates in the context of relationship. So it is no accident that God made humankind with the capacity and need for a relationship. It is part of being created in God's image; He designed us for a relationship. Transformation by the gospel of Jesus Christ has a specific meaning, found in the context of the story of Abraham's household. It is the story of the family of God, revealing the glory of God, driven by the love of God.

In light of this context, transformation is not a generic process of change that results from applying a particular set of principles. It is a state of relatedness in the household of God.

LEAVE AND CLEAVE

The household of God is Abraham and his spiritual descendants,[26] the remnant of all who laid hold of the Blessing. When an individual joins this household, it is an event in history, a birth. Like physical birth, a public ceremony, which we call the believer's baptism, marks the occasion. Baptism in water is a public announcement to the world that a person has left Satan's family and has joined the household of God. When I came to Jesus Christ, I left Satan's family and joined the family of God. Now I have two identities, an old and a new. The single event of leaving Satan's family and cleaving to the household of God is not a change in the status of the old identity; rather, this event marks the death of this old identity and the creation of a new one.

From creation to God's covenant with the patriarchs and onward to the birth of Jesus, the story always progresses in the family context. Notice that it takes considerable study to discern the history of nations or other institutions from the Old Testament. In contrast, the Old Testament recounts the family record repeatedly; it is a clear common thread that runs straight through from beginning to end.[27]

Writers of the New Testament use the phrases "body of Christ" and "the household of God"[28] to show believers how we are related to God and

---

[26] Galatians 3:7, 29.

[27] See all the genealogies listed in Genesis, Leviticus, Numbers, Chronicles, and Matthew and Luke's Gospels.

[28] John 14:2–3; Eph 1:5, 2:19; 1 Tim 3:15.

each other. Hebrews 12 builds on this image by comparing earthly fathers with the heavenly Father.

In the family context, the concept of leaving and cleaving is prominent in the biblical narrative. In the marriage relationship,[29] a man is to leave his father and mother and cleave to his wife. God's covenant with Abraham required him to leave his father's house in Ur of the Chaldeans and go to a place that God would later show him. Salvation, as Jesus explained, meant that one must leave Satan and cleave to God the heavenly Father. Jesus's stern rebuke makes this point clear:

> *Jesus said to them, "If God were your Father, you would love me, for I have come here from God. I have not come on my own; God sent me. Why is my language not clear to you? Because you are unable to hear what I say. You belong to your father, the devil, and you want to carry out your father's desires. He was a murderer from the beginning, not holding to the truth, for there is no truth in him. When he lies, he speaks his native language, for he is a liar and the father of lies. Yet because I tell the truth, you do not believe me! Can any of you prove me guilty of sin? If I am telling the truth, why don't you believe me? Whoever belongs to God hears what God says. The reason you do not hear is that you do not belong to God." — John 8:42–47 NIV*

It cannot be any more explicit than that; salvation is leaving Satan and cleaving to the Father of Jesus Christ. The process of leaving Satan and cleaving to the Father is what I am calling transformation through the gospel of Jesus Christ, and it is possible only through adoption[30] into the family of God. As mentioned earlier, it involves death and birth, brings us into a new community, and bestows a new inheritance.

---

[29] Genesis 2:24.
[30] Ephesians 1:5.

A NEW PATRIARCH

In the household of God, we have a Patriarch and a new identity. Our spirit, which was dead because of our sin, is resurrected to life. And with our spirit, we can hear God and worship Him. Jesus explained to Nicodemus[31] that the rebirth of our spirit is an act of creation that God performs. It is not something we do; just like birth, it is an event that happens once to the individual. With the new identity that we derive from our heavenly Father comes a new relationship with Him that confers on us His holiness. Peter, the apostle, makes the connection for us in his epistle, admonishing us to be holy because our Father in heaven is holy.[32] Like Father, like children; He is holy, so it is normal for His children to be holy as well.

Many years ago, one of our small groups became close friends with someone whose life was transformed by the gospel. She was a single mother and dated several men, but none of them were right for her. They all wanted one thing, and she went along with them, hoping that the relationship would develop. She heard of a group of people meeting at homes on Sundays and asked if she could attend. The group's shepherd invited her to the meeting to share her life story with the others, and she did. At the home group meeting, she said that she, too, was a believer in Jesus Christ. The shepherd asked her, "How can you be a Christian and be involved in intimate relationships outside of marriage?" She didn't see it so black and white but thought maybe there was a gray zone where a believer can live in sin and have forgiveness. The shepherd shared with her an illustration. He said a believer's relationship with God is like a beautiful young princess, dressed in a white wedding gown for her groom. Then he asked her, "Does it make sense for the princess with her white gown to jump into a pig pen and romp in the slop and mud?"

She quickly made the connection, "I am a princess?"

The shepherd answered, "If you are a believer, you most certainly are; you are the daughter of the King of all creation."

The next Sunday, she attended the gathering with her Bible in hand and testified how God spoke to her that she should act as His daughter. From that point on, she ended the intimate relationships with the men she

---

[31] John 3.
[32] 1 Peter 1:16 quoting Leviticus 11.

knew. She waited for some years, and God gave her a wonderful and godly husband. Her transformation began with an embrace of her new identity as the daughter of the King.

Paul's epistle to the Romans sets forth a foundation for transformation through the gospel of Jesus Christ. In the epistle, he urges us to offer ourselves to God as a living and holy sacrifice.[33] The apostle says that we should make this offering because of all the mercies God gave us when He saved us from our iniquity and united us with Jesus Christ in His death, burial, and resurrection. For years, I struggled to be upright, a generous and hospitable man with integrity, which is how my mother described my earthly father. I wanted to be like him but failed. Once I embraced my new identity as a son of God, I started to act like a child of God; my transformed heart consequently transformed my behavior.

FROM MT. HERMON TO JERUSALEM

In 2005 a Palestinian man came to visit at Access. He shared with me his testimony of how he came to know Jesus Christ and how Jesus transformed his life. He was born in a Palestinian camp in Lebanon. In his early twenties, he became a *muezzin*, which means he gave the call to prayer from the mosque's minaret. He was from a low-income family, and life was a struggle for him, as it was for everyone else in the camp. He didn't have a car, so he hitched rides often. On one of the rides, a Lebanese man shared the gospel with him, and in turn, he shared the Quran with the Lebanese man. The trip led to a relationship that culminated three years later in the muezzin coming to faith in Jesus Christ. He grew in his faith and became part of a fellowship of believers led by seasoned servants of Jesus Christ, and they poured a lot of love into his life. He became part of the family and attended their services and conferences regularly.

One gathering was held in Cyprus, a short distance from Lebanon's coast. He and a group of believers went there for four days, and they had some time set aside for tours and recreation. He and another friend used their time to go for a walk around the island. On one of their excursions, they came across a house with a beautifully landscaped front yard, and

---

[33] Romans 12:1.

they decided to take some pictures on the lawn. They stepped onto the property and started snapping phone cameras. A man came out of the house and asked them what they were doing, and when they told him, he was amiable and invited them inside. The two accepted the invitation and walked into the house to find a group of twelve people there. It turned out that they were Messianic Jews who had flown in from Israel to have a time of teaching and prayer together. Can you imagine the situation? Two Palestinians from Lebanon joined twelve Jews from Israel, all having traveled to Cyprus to go deeper with Jesus.

What he told me next brought tears to my eyes. He said that when the people inside found out who they were, they embraced them, brought out bowls of water, took their shoes and socks off, and washed their feet! Yes, that happened. The two Palestinians went back to their leaders and told them the story; the next day, a group of Lebanese went to the same house and washed the feet of the Messianic Jews. With tears, they asked forgiveness on behalf of their people and prayed for reconciliation of the Jews and Arabs. This testimony has to be one of the most powerful examples I have heard of the power of the gospel of Jesus Christ to transform communities.

Here is what the apostle Paul says in his letter to the Ephesians about peace, something that I believe holds the answer to resolving the Arab–Israeli conflict:

> Don't forget that you Gentiles used to be outsiders. You were called "uncircumcised heathens" by the Jews, who were proud of their circumcision, even though it affected only their bodies and not their hearts. In those days you were living apart from Christ. You were excluded from citizenship among the people of Israel, and you did not know the covenant promises God had made to them. You lived in this world without God and without hope. But now you have been united with Christ Jesus. Once you were far away from God, but now you have been brought near to him through the blood of Christ.
>
> For Christ himself has brought peace to us. He united Jews and Gentiles into one people when, in his own body on the

cross, he broke down the wall of hostility that separated us. He did this by ending the system of law with its commandments and regulations. He made peace between Jews and Gentiles by creating in himself one new people from the two groups. Together as one body, Christ reconciled both groups to God by means of his death on the cross, and our hostility toward each other was put to death.

— Ephesians 2:11–16

When people come to Jesus Christ, they become one family. Joining His family does not require a certain genetic pedigree or a specific heritage. It requires only faith in Jesus. The death of Jesus Christ on the cross reconciles Jews and Arabs today when they both embrace Him. It is a simple message, and I have seen it work.

I have noticed a pattern among those who come to Christ in the Middle East; after a few months with the Lord, they start asking themselves and others questions about what the Bible says about Israel. Gradually, as they read more and experience Jesus's presence in their lives, they start to lose their hatred toward people, including Israelis, and become more willing to accommodate them. I have heard several testimonies from Palestinians and Jews who live together in peace in Jerusalem, offering each other shelter from persecution after they come to faith. One believer told me that he lived for several weeks with a family of Messianic Jews who hid him from his physical family; they wanted to kill him for believing in Jesus Christ. Likewise, I have heard testimonies of Messianic Jews who took shelter with Palestinian believers to escape persecution from their families. The answer to the Arab–Israeli conflict is for both people groups to come to Jesus, and my prayer and vision is that one day all of them will become one in Him.

One day, I was alone on top of Baruk Mountain in Lebanon, looking over the Beqaa valley and Mt. Hermon in the distance. I was praying for the nations, and the Lord spoke to me through Psalm 133:

How wonderful and pleasant it is
when brothers live together in harmony!
For harmony is as precious as the anointing oil

that was poured over Aaron's head,
that ran down his beard
and onto the border of his robe.
Harmony is as refreshing as the dew from Mount Hermon
that falls on the mountains of Zion.
And there the Lord has pronounced his blessing,
even life everlasting. — Psalm 133:1–3

The anointing oil on Aaron's body and the dew of Hermon are symbols of the Holy Spirit. Aaron is a symbol of Israel, and the psalm speaks of David's dream that someday the Holy Spirit would anoint all Israel, from head to toe. The Lord graced my heart with a thought. The dew descending on Hermon represents the Holy Spirit descending the mountain, gathering in streams of revival and feeding into the Sea of Galilee, then flowing along the Jordan River down to Mt. Zion in Jerusalem. Hundreds of thousands of Druze, Orthodox Christians, and Muslims inhabit Mt. Hermon's foothills. I prayed for them that the Holy Spirit would descend on them and carry the good news to all people from Mt. Hermon to Jerusalem.

God inspired King David with the love story in Psalm 133, of harmony and revival flowing across the region, and I pray to be able to see it unfold one day. In God's book, the Arabs and the Jews are a blessing to one another. The recent Abraham Accords have started a political and economic peace process between the Arabs and Israel. If these accords are genuinely Abrahamic, they must include both sides making peace with the God of Abraham, Isaac, and Jacob.

One Sunday morning, I sat in a Sunday School class to listen to a man with a Ph.D. in theology. His lesson was on the life of Abraham, and he set anchor at the conception of Ishmael. He said, "Imagine what it would have been like if Ishmael were never born. There would be no Arabs today, and we'd have no conflict in the Middle East." Wouldn't that be nice? He went on a long discourse of how the whole Arab–Israeli conflict could have been avoided had Abraham and Sarah not acted in the flesh. He paid no attention to God's sovereignty and could not conceive that God meant it for good. How is the life of Ishmael any different from the experience of Joseph, who said of the envy and betrayal by his brothers, "They meant it for evil, but God meant it for good"? Joseph was a blessing to Israel, wasn't he? And so is Ishmael.

Sadly, I hear this bigotry against the Arabs from many believers in Jesus. They think that to bless Israel, they must curse the Arabs. I want to offer a gentle rebuke to those who think this way. This attitude is not from the Lord. The Arabs are not a mistake; they are a prized creation of God, and Jesus laid down His life for them, just as He did for you. Don't let your love for Israel translate into scorn for the Arabs.

CHAPTER THREE
THE NEED FOR TRANSFORMATION

Transformation by the gospel of Jesus Christ is about being made into the person that God intended you to be. As your creator, He made you one of a kind, a unique design; there is no one like you in the whole world—not in the past, not now, and not in the future. Only God knows you inside and out, and you need Him to reveal this to you. Other people, even your parents who brought you to this world, don't truly know you because they didn't design you. You don't know who you are either; all your life, as you grow, you will continue along a journey of self-discovery. Since God has the blueprint for your design, He also knows exactly how you will be transformed into the person He created you to be. Are you ready to begin this process of transformation?

In recent years, the word transformation has become quite popular. Marketing companies advertise products that promise to transform our lives. The world's need for change has never been more evident. We seek relief from something—debt, depression, loneliness, sickness, pain, or the like—and we want the key that will bring about change from the status quo. As we mature and develop a deeper understanding of human history and our current state, we realize that we must change not only on an individual level but as societies in general.

My wife and I recently watched a movie called *The Promise*. It is a story about an Armenian doctor from Turkey and an American reporter covering the region's news. Through their stories, the movie documents the horrific genocide of Turkey's Armenians in a personal and heart-wrenching drama.[34] The film caused us to look further into the Armenian genocide, summarized well in a New York Times article by John Kifner.[35] According to Kifner, the Young Turk movement emerged due to a resurgence of Islamic religious sentiment. They gained control of the crumbling Ottoman Empire in 1908 and sided with Germany in World War I. The Armenians, who are Christians, sided with the Russians, which helped the Young Turks build a case against them and precipitated their genocide and expulsion from Turkey. One and a half million Armenians who were living in East Turkey were massacred. Rape, killing, and forced exodus to the Syrian desert without water or supplies, labeled "deportation" by the government, were the salient methods employed in the genocide. The Armenians who made it through the desert settled in different parts of Lebanon and Syria and formed communities that integrated the local culture well.

Armenians in the Levant[36] identify themselves as Syrian or Lebanese and are quite patriotic and involved in their new country's political and social life. They are known for their skills in manufacturing and industry and are valued for their excellent work ethic. They also guarded their Armenian culture, contributing beautifully to the cultural bouquet that is the Levant. We have many Armenian friends and coworkers in Lebanon. We often pray for them for healing and freedom from the emotional, psychological, and sometimes even spiritual bondage that the genocide has brought upon them.

Unfortunately, from Old Testament times until now, ethnic cleansing and genocide have been a painful reality, one that has haunted every cultural majority. Humanity's conscience is burdened by the weight of shame we have amassed over the centuries, yet in every case of genocide, the

---

[34] Miriam-Webster Dictionary defines ethnic cleansing as "the expulsion, imprisonment, or killing of an ethnic minority by a dominant majority to achieve ethnic homogeneity." Genocide has as its goal "the extermination of an ethnic group"; thus, it is an extreme form of ethnic cleansing.

[35] John Kifner, "Armenian Genocide of 1915: An Overview," New York Times, accessed June 3, 2020, retrieved from archive.nytimes.com/www.nytimes.com/ref/timestopics/topics_armeniangenocide. html?mcubz=3.

[36] The Levant is a region that encompasses Lebanon, Syria, Jordan, Israel, and Palestine.

perpetrators have felt justified in their actions. This sentiment is certainly true in the ongoing worldwide genocide of unborn babies. This atrocity is generally not recognized as genocidal but as "freedom of choice" to take a life. As I consider recorded history, it is evident that every civilization is built on the ashes of another, and genocides are a recurring theme in the process. Abortion alone has put to death over 60 million babies since 1973. In the last hundred years, there have been fifty-one documented genocides worldwide, with a death toll of 58 million people; we have seen the Holocaust, the Holodomor, and slaughters in Armenia, Cambodia, Rwanda, Bosnia, and Darfur.

Genocide is an extreme expression of a seemingly benign worldview known as ethnocentricity. Every person has a preferred way of doing things, and consequently, we favor our culture. There is no problem with favoring our culture, but it becomes a problem when we start comparing and despising other cultures. Ethnocentricity is the belief that our way is better, and we assume that what is good for us must be suitable for others.

RELIGION

A full understanding of the root cause of genocide and the human propensity for ethnic cleansing is elusive. Academia may point to war, history, economics, and public opinion as the main forces that forge this mass human behavior, but there is more to it than that. I believe that the human desire for "cleansing" goes beyond ethnicity and is rooted in a deep sense of self-righteousness. Genocide is rooted in religion, the epitome of intolerance to anyone with a different faith.

Religion, the way I understand it, is an expression of a person's deep conviction of self-righteousness; religion says that one garners God's favor by belonging to the right group and practicing the tenets it prescribes. This self-righteousness evolves into a convenient tool by which one can justify practically any behavior based on the moment's circumstances. As a human construct of thought and practice, religion requires defense against those who would disprove its value or validity.

There are varieties of well-known religions globally: Christianity, Islam, Buddhism, Hinduism, Confucianism, etc. But there are also many clandestine religions that are rarely categorized as such, like atheism, communism, capitalism, environmentalism, conservatism, liberalism, and hedonism; yes, I believe these are religions and the nurseries of the "cleansing" instinct.

James identifies the source of violence and conflict in the world:

> *What is causing the quarrels and fights among you? Don't they come from the evil desires at war within you? You want what you don't have, so you scheme and kill to get it. You are jealous of what others have, but you can't get it, so you fight and wage war to take it away from them. Yet you don't have what you want because you don't ask God for it. And even when you ask, you don't get it because your motives are all wrong—you want only what will give you pleasure.*
> *— James 4:1–3*

The verses outline a pathway from individual selfishness to war, and history shows that the path binds all nations and cultures. It is a spectrum that connects personal attitudes to mass movements, revealing a destructive cycle that has oppressed humanity throughout history.

We don't have to wait to reach the genocidal stages to realize that we must change. Take the US for an example. The country is severely divided by political rhetoric; the media spins stories to recruit support for a party. The resulting bias drives people toward leftist movements like Antifa and Black Lives Matter or Proud Boys and other supremacist groups on the extreme right. Religion demands proselytization, which makes for a tense coexistence of different groups. This demand is why zealot movements and awakenings spring up periodically throughout human history, peaking when one group becomes a majority over another, in an ongoing cycle of violence and hostility. We look at the Islamic conquests and the Christian Crusades as the most famous examples, but religious violence continues to afflict communities worldwide.

I have often heard ministers repeat the axiom, "Religion is man's attempt to reach God, and Christianity is God's attempt to reach man." It explains well the difference between religion and faith in Jesus Christ.

Considering that the gospel's ultimate goal is to reveal God's righteousness,[37] religions have undertaken to corrupt it. They mask the revelation of God in an unholy mixture of pious legalism.[38] For millennia, religions have come against the Kingdom of God, unsuccessfully attempting to contain, isolate, and extinguish the gospel of Jesus Christ. The gospel is breaking out all over the Earth amid great hostility and resistance against the real revelation of God.

CULTURE

As a Lebanese American, I have a cross-cultural life, directly sensing the opposing forces at work in my two cultures. Being attracted to each one separately, I experience a mixed bag of love and disappointment and feel the need for transformation in both.

For my American culture, I have a deep love for the value it places on the individual and the inalienable rights of equality, and all the freedoms that proceed from that core value. I also love the work ethic and the extraordinary generosity shown toward the needy and the stranger among us. But some things must change, such as the loneliness that people experience in this land of rugged individualism. There is also an imbalance in life that results from blind adoration of organizational methods by which everything ticks toward an economic goal. The economic machine has a dehumanizing effect on the individual and can create a void in people's hearts in this culture.

Another reason we need a transformation in America is to turn away from our violent tendencies. A string of bloody wars marks our nation's history, making us responsible for much suffering at home and abroad; we need look no further than our mistreatment of the Native American population in the last two centuries. In these and many other situations, we still need healing and reconciliation. But resolving these issues will put us on the road to a transformed society. Another alarming trend is the widening political and cultural divide that has overtaken politics in the US, and it is tearing the country apart. Hypocrisy and intolerance are

---

[37] Romans 1:17.
[38] 2 Timothy 3:1–5.

rampant among the liberal and conservative factions, making it almost impossible to work together. The American culture is in great need of redemption and transformation.

As for my Lebanese culture, I have a deep love for the security and belonging that come from my extended family. I also like how easy it is for us to make friends and develop life-long relationships. But the Lebanese culture has deep-rooted sectarianism that builds insurmountable walls between people groups. It conscripts the individual to serve within the confines of their ethnic or religious group. It can be suffocating. I am also very disappointed in how we have clung to so much hatred for so long, preventing any prospect of real national unity without tyrannical rule. People and cultures of the Middle East are in desperate need of transformation.

As a result of my study of the Bible and my experience in two cultures, I believe that all cultures are thoroughly and intrinsically defective. I learned that culture itself is neither right nor wrong during my formal education, but I have since come to doubt that claim seriously. Humans have all delved deeply into the darkness of religion and self-righteousness. These have manifested in every culture; therefore, since cultures are the emergence of human behavior, they will undoubtedly reflect the sin in humans. Culture is the collection of behaviors that a given group of people has found acceptable and normal. It cannot be separated or exonerated from our corporate crime. I have looked for the "correct" culture and have yet to find it. Were I to declare my own culture correct, I would be perpetuating the denial of our collective shame and helping to enable the next "justified cleansing."

With the views I have presented here, I am sure I have managed to offend people in both of my cultures and have given them ample reason to reject me and my perspective. But it was never my intent to offend or attack either one because my love for both is genuine, and I don't advocate a cynical attitude toward either one. I am writing on transformation because I have found hope.

I believe that we have one hope for deliverance from the shame of our culture. It is the Kingdom of God through the gospel of Jesus Christ. As revealed in the Bible, the Kingdom of God is not a religion at all. The Kingdom was proclaimed in Jerusalem two thousand years ago as a rebuke and a condemnation of the religious institutions of the time. These institutions recognized the Kingdom as a significant threat to their very existence and have been trying to extinguish the gospel ever since.

In the Middle East, sectarian lines are drawn, and a seemingly cordial yet cold coexistence covers the dark hatred for each other that lurks underneath. Hostility is pressurized and ready to explode at the slightest imbalance or ripple in the political landscape. Like vicious wolves unleashed, majority sects of the Middle East have devoured the minorities around them and have morphed into geographical blocs of conforming ethnicities. Jews together, Sunnis together, Shia together, and a sprinkling of minorities among them. Christianity has been expelled from the region. The Middle East is fortified against outside cultures and religions and very resistant to the gospel.

Yet, there is an example of a transformation that began a few years ago. Despite the seemingly insurmountable hostility and enmity, the Druze of Lebanon and Syria have whole-heartedly and openly received the gospel of Jesus Christ. It grew from within the culture, not as a foreign intrusion, but as an answer to the Druze's hopes and aspirations to know God personally and make Him known. Many of them see the Bible as their book, and their walk with God is the natural outcome of being children in the household of God. They have established a transformed community called The Lord's Family and Access International School. This expression of the gospel is a radical departure from religion, and as more and more people seek to flee the grasp of religion's enslavement, it guides them to find refuge in the Kingdom of God. Within the fortified walls of the non-Christian communities of Lebanon and Syria, The Lord's Family is a place of refuge for those seeking the Kingdom of God. Here captives are set free from sin and darkness, from their genocidal history, and the self-righteousness of religion.

Religion is the reason we need transformation not only in the Middle East but worldwide. In the US, churches are suffering from religiosity and a shallow expression of faith in Jesus Christ. The best music, preaching, and facilities that man can put together have not transformed people into disciples of Jesus Christ. Over the past hundred years, the church in the US has produced a consumerist version of the gospel, and changed lives are not part of it for most congregations.

Transformation is an elusive goal. The word is part of the mission statements of many churches because they realize something is missing. According to the Bible, if anyone can deliver transformation, it should be those of us within the Church. It is the reason God put us here. Sadly, we are not performing on the transformation front as we should. Churches are searching for discipleship programs and material that will help their congregations obey Romans 12:2, which commands us, "Do not be conformed to this world but be transformed by the renewing of our minds." But are we looking in the right places?

TRANSFORMATION IS A PROBLEM FOR THE CHURCH

I met James at a men's Bible study group and got to know him and his wife well. James was a brilliant software engineer, and companies were lining up to give him projects. He was making so much money that he decided to work on weekends only and take the rest of the week off. Faith in Jesus Christ and a desire to obey the Word of God formed a common bond between us, so we had many good conversations. In time, his wife began sharing with me a detail about their lives that was disturbing: She told me that he was addicted to drugs. I was stunned and didn't know if I should believe her; he looked so successful and seemed to have a sincere desire to walk with God. One day, she called me and asked me if I had seen her husband. She said he had been missing for two days, and she didn't know where he went. The next day I called to check on him, and she told me that the police had found his dead body in an abandoned building. The cause of death was a drug overdose.

The devastating end to his life raised a question in my mind about the gospel of Jesus Christ. Here is a man who said he believed in Jesus Christ. He studied the Bible, prayed, and was a member of a church that he attended regularly. How could he be addicted to drugs? He and his wife prayed and called out to God, asking for deliverance from his addiction. Why was he not changed? The answers I received from pastors and teachers of the Bible were more puzzling than the questions. They said that some believers are still carnal or immature; their experience has not yet risen to the level of their position in Christ. One can explain anything and everything with such an answer, making God's promises somewhat arbitrary; sometimes they work, and other times they don't.

To say that some believers are transformed while others are not reflects negatively on our faith and raises a new set of questions. What makes faith in Jesus unique? How is it different from any other religion that speaks of high ideals but makes no difference in real life? Why was my friend's life not transformed, and what could he have done differently? This story is not unique or rare in the Church. Sadly, it is a common occurrence.

Media reports say that church membership does not affect the likelihood of broken families and marriages[39] or suicide.[40] They say that being a church member does not significantly change the individual's quality of life. Such a serious charge against the Church leaves unanswered questions in the minds of young investigators who are seeking the Truth. Millennials want to see faith in action, not only doctrine. Many are asking, "What makes Christianity different from Islam, Buddhism, or any other religion?"

Believers in Jesus Christ are in a constant struggle, yearning to walk in the Spirit. But living the transformed life is not easy, so many settle for a compromise and do the best with what they have. Others get discouraged and give up because they don't see tangible results of their faith in Christ. As a shepherd of God's people, I am always frustrated with the sin-ravaged lives of believers. Satan is waging war against the church and winning too many battles.

The church has suffered disunity, slander, bitterness, immorality, greed, envy, and back-stabbing. In my experience planting churches in the Middle East, the fiercest opposition and persecution came from within the church, not the world. I know many people who professed faith in Jesus Christ but never experienced the life-changing power of His gospel. They attended worship services on Sundays and learned church lingo but ultimately walked away from the faith. In the late nineties, a believer came to me and said that she decided to leave the church. I met with her

---

[39] "New Marriage and Divorce Statistics Released," Barna, March 31, 2008, accessed June 23, 2020, from www.barna.com/research/new-marriage-and-divorce-statistics-released/.

[40] Sarah Eekhoff Zylstra, "Why Pastors Are Committing Suicide," The Gospel Coalition, November 23, 2016, accessed June 23, 2020, from www.thegospelcoalition.org/article/why-pastors-are- committing-suicide/.

to find out why, and all she could say was, "It is too difficult to fake it in this church." After the meeting, I turned to my wife and said, "There goes another church attender." I lost count of all the church attenders who came and went over the past two decades, but I am sure they are many. Walt Henrichson's booklet "Many Aspire, Few Attain"[41] shares this harsh reality of Christian ministry, and my experience affirms it is true. It is sobering to consider that most people in our congregations in the US and Europe are merely church attenders.

The Reformation that began with Zwingli and Luther ca. 1517 was based on their agreement that Scripture, not the Pope, is the highest authority in the Church. On this basis, they affirmed that justification is by grace alone, not by works, and they developed a language for the gospel as a message of salvation. However, the Reformation leaders did not produce a unified doctrine of sanctification and the relationship between grace and works.[42] As a result, the language that developed to communicate the process of the believer's transformation was varied and not easy to communicate.

This difference shows up in our current perspective of justification and sanctification. Most people in western culture are familiar with the imperative "Get saved!" When we read it, we understand what it means right away. It's talking about the gospel of Jesus Christ and a person's decision to receive Him as Lord and Savior. This concise message developed over the centuries makes it immediately recognizable by most people in the Western hemisphere, and it is easy to pass on to others. Not so with transformation. It is not obvious that the phrase "Be transformed!" is talking about change by the gospel of Jesus Christ. Evangelicals have developed a clear message of salvation by grace through faith alone, apart from works, and made it clear, but they have yet to do the same with sanctification or the process of transformation.

Theologians present salvation as a three-pronged event: justification,

---

[41] Discipleship Library, 2007, accessed June 23, 2020, from www.discipleshiplibrary.com/pdfs/ G208.pdf.

[42] Will Graham, "10 Differences Between Luther and Zwingli: How to Differentiate Between the Two Protestant Reformers?" Evangelical Focus, August 3, 2019, accessed June 4, 2020, retrieved from evangelicalfocus.com/magazine/4647/10_differences_between_Luther_and_Zwingli.

sanctification, and glorification. These are organized along a timeline, beginning with the new spiritual birth, continuing with sanctification, and fully realized at the second coming of Jesus Christ, when we will join Him in glory. This framework conceives transformation as the next phase after getting saved, and so it treats it as a separate issue.

Bible study designs reflect such a perception; the depth of teaching varies to meet the participants' perceived needs. Some Bible studies are evangelistic, others facilitate basic discipleship, and still others provide leadership training. If a disciple continues to hunger for teaching, we may encourage the pursuit of seminary education. This setup can be useful, but it can also give a false impression that these are "levels" that a person achieves with added knowledge and effort, which is inherently misleading.

The desire to follow this prescribed progression through levels of achievement creates an unhelpful pressure. Since trainees cannot proceed to the next level unless they complete the one before it, lack of spiritual growth can cause them to drop out of the program or hide their struggles from the group. After missing too many "quiet times," falling behind in the daily reading program, not bringing new people into the group, or returning to old habitual sin, it becomes clear to the trainees that they are not experiencing transformation as they ought to. When this happens, they perceive that their transformation program has failed somehow, so to remain faithful and committed to the faith, they defer their expectation of transformation later. They enter a waiting mode, often called the desert experience, wondering where God is leading them. Some may give up on discipleship and transformation altogether and settle for a "sit, soak, and sleep" role in the church. Others may undertake extraordinary tasks in the hope of laying hold of what they consider to be an elusive experience of being transformed by the gospel of Jesus Christ.

The view of transformation as a timeline also affects how we appoint leaders in the church; we select those who succeed in the prescribed program and get results. But there is a problem with such a system even when the trainees do well. Success defined by the prescribed program becomes the way calling and leadership are determined, and we neglect to seek God's leading. So we end up with leaders whom, though deemed capable by human standards, God has not necessarily appointed.

It is noteworthy that Jesus did not frame His teaching in the same pattern as our usual Bible study series and leadership development programs. He started with a passage that applies to people everywhere—the Sermon on the Mount. The teaching is not separated into levels or a sequence of accomplishments; it simply contains facets of the core message. In this sermon, Jesus teaches justification, discipleship, and leadership in every verse, all at once. Our concise formulation of the gospel as a message of salvation is only part of the Sermon on the Mount. What we leave out is the transformational dimension of the gospel.[43]

Although transformation is at the heart of the gospel, our message of salvation focuses on laying hold of heaven's blessing and eternal life. We tend to overlook or postpone the critical transformation that God desires to perform in us.

TRANSFORMATION IS THE HALLMARK OF THE GOSPEL

Transformation is not an added option to the gospel of Jesus Christ, but of its essence. The gospel is a message that speaks of God's love for us, and it gives us a look at His thoughts and character, as well as ours. One of the clearest of such examinations comes from the book of Isaiah.

> *The Spirit of the Sovereign Lord is upon me,*
> *for the Lord has anointed me*
> *to bring good news to the poor.*
>
> *He has sent me to comfort the brokenhearted*
> *and to proclaim that captives will be released*
> *and prisoners will be freed.*
>
> *He has sent me to tell those who mourn*
> *that the time of the Lord's favor has come,*
> *and with it, the day of God's anger*
> *against their enemies.*

---

[43] It is possible that the Western analytical approach to Scripture, of breaking systems into manageable components, analyzing each separately, and then reassembling them to form a model gospel message, is what led to this lack of understanding of transformation.

To all who mourn in Israel,
he will give a crown of beauty for ashes,
a joyous blessing instead of mourning,
festive praise instead of despair.

In their righteousness, they will be like great oaks
that the Lord has planted for his own glory.

— *Isaiah 61:1–3*

Jesus used this passage to reveal Himself to the people of Nazareth when He spoke at the synagogue. He also used it as an outline for His Sermon on the Mount. He said that the Father sent Him to save the poor in spirit, making it clear that He is talking about a spiritual transformation, not only a physical one. The table below outlines the state of the poor in spirit according to Isaiah 61 and describes the change that Jesus brings to make them into oaks of righteousness:

The State of Being Poor in Spirit	The State of Being Oaks of Righteousness
Brokenhearted: Our hearts break because of death, loss, betrayal, fear, injustice, lust, addictions.	Comforted: Hope, healing, consolation.
Captive: Imprisoned by sin and darkness of the soul.	Free from sin: The privilege to do what is right in God's eyes—walking in the light.
Mourning: Grieving over losses suffered in life. In the Old Testament times, people expressed grief by sprinkling ashes on their heads and not grooming themselves for the period of mourning.	Joyful: Cleansing makes the person look and feel beautiful. The gospel is grooming after a period of neglect. It is like pouring perfume on the head.
Despair: There is no hope.	Celebration: Lifting praise to God.

Every verse shows the process of transformation from one state to another. According to verse 3, God transforms us into oaks of righteousness to put us on display for all creation to see, and then they will respond with praise to Him. It has always impressed me that the gospel's ultimate goal is the glory of God, not our salvation. Isn't that something? It's not all about us. Yes, God loves us so much that He sent His one and only Son to die for us. But even so, there is Someone more important and more worthy than ourselves. This perspective helps me, especially in times of suffering, to focus on what truly matters in eternity. While he was in prison chains, the apostle Paul said that he is not ashamed of the gospel because it reveals God's righteousness (Romans 1:17). He ignored his chains and kept his eyes on the glory that God was receiving in his imprisonment.

Transformation results in visible evidence of the power of the gospel. Luke 5:17–26 tells of the story of a paralyzed man whose friends lowered him through the roof into the room where Jesus was teaching. They had to go through the roof because the crowds wouldn't let them through. Jesus looked at the man and said, "Young man, your sins are forgiven." Then he added, "So I will prove to you that the Son of Man has the authority on earth to forgive sins." Then Jesus turned to the paralyzed man and said, "Stand up, pick up your mat, and go home!" The gospel of salvation through Jesus Christ came with physical proof, a change from sickness to health, from bondage to freedom.

In the spiritual realm, the gospel of Jesus Christ advances on a battlefield. Knowledge of theology alone is not sufficient in this showdown—it is an Elijah versus the prophets of Baal–type of confrontation, and the one with proof wins the day. This proof can be a miracle from God or a sign; in Elijah's case, fire descended from heaven and consumed Elijah's sacrifice as the people watched. Yet, though it is hard to believe, people quickly forget such proof. Historians and media pundits can "hijack" the story and attribute it to their prophet of choice. Many attribute stories of healings, visions, and dreams to the Virgin Mary or other saints and prophets and the result is that these are no longer exclusively signs of the gospel. The world can imitate them and present its rendition of "proof."

Having worked in the Middle East for two decades, I am aware of the stories of dreams and visions told by people who came to Jesus from Islamic backgrounds. I am sure that some are sincere, but different religions make similar claims. Signs and miracles are the primary fodder for religious marketing in the Middle East. It doesn't mean that the miracles that God performs in the lives of many are invalid. It means that their attribution to the gospel is somehow watered down or muddled by different groups.

Like Pharaoh's magicians, the world can match some signs and wonders used by God's people as evidence of His power. But one distinctive is unique to the gospel of Jesus Christ, and the world cannot match it. It's the transformation of a believer, the most visible and effective testimony of the gospel.

In October 2013, hundreds of families of Syrian refugees came to our school's neighborhood in Lebanon. Access International School is a Christian school where we teach the Bible and introduce students, parents, and staff to a personal relationship with Jesus Christ. The refugees arrived with nothing, just the clothes on their backs—some didn't even have shoes. They lived quite comfortably in their homes just a few hours before but suddenly had to f lee from the war. We had anticipated such a scenario several months earlier. We had already purchased hundreds of kilograms of grains, canned foods, staples, and cleaning products, so we packaged them in boxes and delivered them to the refugees. Some of them were living in tents, and others were in small rooms in the parking areas of residential buildings. We included an Arabic Bible in each box and handed it to them, saying, "This is from Jesus." The next week several of them came to the school and asked if Jesus was in His office because they'd like to meet Him and say thank you. We had to explain who Jesus is, and then they understood better what we were saying. We became known as the Christians who were giving out aid to the refugees, and hundreds of people came to the school to ask for help. The need was so great we decided to focus our effort on families within a circle of about a one-kilometer radius around our school.

We had to turn down all who lived outside the radius, but the ones inside were 155 families[44]. For several months we provided weekly grocery rations, blankets, heaters, diesel fuel, socks, shoes, hats, gloves, diapers, and so on. Believers in England, Switzerland, Germany, the US, and Beirut

---

[44] Syrians within the circle were texting their friends and families, telling them to move near the Christian school, which would take care of them.

joined in the effort by providing us with items to distribute. Some ladies at a church in England hand-knitted some wool gloves and socks, which we distributed to the refugees. Several doctors and nurses from our school and other organizations came to help by holding clinics in our chapel. God miraculously provided excellent care for our 155 families. We held regular meetings for these families at our chapel and shared the gospel with them, and most responded very politely with gratitude for what we have done for them.

Figure 1. Gathering at Access waiting for food and diesel distribution.

At one meeting, attended by about 180 adults, we asked them to list what they needed most. With some guidance, they came up with a list of the five most important things they needed at the time: jobs, housing, healthcare, education, and security. We told them we couldn't help them with housing or security but would help with the other three. Classic social undercurrents were driving the meeting. Leaders from among the refugees started popping up, and they were trying to form a consensus opinion. The most vocal leader stood up and said, "Enough of this aid from the Christians; the mosque in the other neighborhood is giving out groceries as well. Let us go to our own people."[45] Another lady stood up and said,

---

[45] He meant the neighborhood mosque.

"A Muslim non-profit organization is coming from Tripoli this weekend to distribute food and hold a medical clinic at city hall." At this, the heads of about ninety families got up and left the chapel. The heads of sixty-five families remained in the room with us. Their leader said, "We want to stay with the Christians because we have never seen this kind of love anywhere before. I have been to the mosque; they treated me like an animal and made me feel like a beggar. Not these Christians. They treated me with love, saying, 'We all need help sometimes.'" Later, as it turned out, neither the mosque nor the non-profit from Tripoli kept their promises. We did, and this act of mercy remains a strong testimony among our local refugees.

Communities of believers worldwide sent money and clothing, while those who worked directly with the refugees served and prayed for them. The Holy Spirit translated these offerings into faith and glory to God among the Syrian refugees.

Miracles of healing, signs, dreams, and wonders are exhilarating and sometimes give clear witness to the power of God. Still, more effective than even these, believers' transformed lives are the most powerful witness I have encountered. People can argue doctrine, but they cannot refute a personal testimony of a life changed by the gospel of Jesus Christ. As John saw and testified, "They have defeated him [Satan] by the blood of the Lamb and by their testimony. And they did not love their lives so much that they were afraid to die" (Revelation 12:11). Our ministry experience in the Middle East shows that a transformed life is the most powerful witness to the salvation that Jesus Christ offers. As ministers in the Church, we want people to profess faith in Jesus, but we want to see their lives transformed by Him even more.

GOD WANTS TO TRANSFORM US

A third reason to focus on transformation is that it's something God desires in the believer. In John 4:24, Jesus says that God the Father is seeking true worshippers who will worship Him in spirit and truth. God has made it clear that He desires intimate and loving fellowship with His people; He wants us to come into His presence individually and as a community. It is a theme that runs through the whole Bible, from the time He asked Adam, "Where are you?" to the time of the patriarchs, the law, and now the Church. In Revelation, John describes how saints from every nation and tongue gather in worship, giving us a taste of heaven. At the end of time, God's plan consummates with His people gathered to worship at His throne.[46] Some Bible scholars teach that when Jesus used Isaiah 61 at the synagogue in Nazareth, it was to proclaim the beginning of His earthly ministry (Luke 4:18). They note that He stopped the quote in the middle of the second verse, which declares the year of the Lord's favor and excludes the phrase about God's wrath against His enemies. This exclusion, they say, indicates that the first coming of Jesus Christ has fulfilled the first half of the verse and that the second coming will fulfill the second half. This observation is important because, if true, we must ask the question, how much transformation should take place now, and how much at the second coming? The Bible teaches us that our transformation will not be complete until the consummation of ages. For example, scholars accurately point out that the gospel has freed us from the power of sin in our current state. Still, a time is coming when we will be relieved of its presence as well. Our transformation is a work in progress, and it is not finished until the body of Christ is complete in number and character.

I have outlined three reasons to study and intentionally aim for transformation. It is a problem area for the Church, something that all believers long for but find hard to attain. It is a hallmark of the gospel and a witness that sets it apart from all other faiths. And finally, it is what God desires for His Church.

---

[46] In his book Let the Nations Be Glad, John Piper shares the now-famous quote, "Missions exist because worship doesn't." One key thought to note here is that he uses the word "missions" with an s, not mission. There is only one Mission of God, yet many missions in service to that goal. These missions establish the missionary calling of the Church on the foundation of God's nature as one who reaches out and communicates. In this sense, God's Mission and the worship that Piper is speaking of are the same. God's Mission is to reveal His glory to all creation, and in response, all creation worships Him. His act of revealing His glory is the very foundation of the missionary outreach of the Church.

CHAPTER FOUR
TWO KINDS OF TRANSFORMATION

From the moment we are born, our bodies are changing, growing, and getting older, so in a sense, transformation applies to all life. The word transformation means "a thorough or dramatic change in form or appearance."[47] The Oxford English Dictionary also includes more extended definitions; among them are mathematical transformation and genetic transformation. The word can have different meanings and uses depending on the context, which is why I need to elaborate on what it means in the context of faith in Jesus Christ.

There is one kind of transformation that the world offers, and I call it transformation through conformity. Another is what the Bible reveals as God's work in us; I call it transformation through creation.

TRANSFORMATION THROUGH CONFORMITY

Transformation through conformity assumes that real change happens by changing actions or modifying behavior to conform to a predetermined standard. This kind of transformation is what we are used to in everyday life. The government expects us to conform to the law, a school expects us to meet a standard to get a degree, and the military trains soldiers to

---

[47] Oxford University Press, Lexico.com, 2019.

reach a standard it sets. The basic setup is that there is a mold in which we cast the person, and we apply pressure through surrounding forces to conform them to the shape of the shell. Then we wait for a predetermined period, and out pops the transformed product. The mold produces what the system requires, whatever it may be, whether an engineer, a father or mother, a soldier, a terrorist, a consumer, and so on. Force is applied by the prevailing circumstances and events in which the subject lives.

I was part of a group of people who met in Istanbul to implement scenario planning methodology in our company. Scenario Planning[48] is a tool developed by Shell Oil Corporation to foresee all possible future scenarios and prepare the company for each of them. Then as life unfolds, one can see which scenario is playing out and implement the appropriate action plan. It is sheer genius. In one part of the scenario planning process, we had to determine the main forces that drive change globally; this would allow us to design different scenarios based on various combinations of these forces' magnitudes. Our group concluded that world events are shaped by three main forces: military power, economics, and public opinion. Different groups and entities throughout the world are using one or more of these forces to transform others into the image they are advocating. Liberals, conservatives, woke, bigoted, globalist, nationalist, feminist, Christian, Muslim, secular, atheist—there is a mold for each of these. At any given moment, many different forces are actively working to squeeze you into one of these molds to turn you into a supporter of a particular movement or product. These are the forces that shape the world.

Transformation by conformity does yield results, and they can even be positive, but they are temporary. It is only a matter of time before the paradigm shifts again, and a new change is needed, making those who were shaped by an old mold obsolete. The world has grown to view leadership as managing the process of change through shifts in geopolitics, markets, or culture. It works from the outside, like an exoskeleton that constrains actions. It applies enough force to keep whatever is inside a person from influencing the outward performance.[49] The result is a relatively functional

---

[48] Muhammad Amer, Tugrul U. Daim, and Antonie Jetter, "A Review of Scenario Planning," Futures, 2013.

[49] This reminds me of the brilliant definition of politics as hate management.

operating system called an organization. This model aims for efficiency and growth. Sadly, it ignores the individual's heart and soul, reducing a person to a component performing in a machine—no inner healing or freedom for the individual or the community is possible within this system. Over time, dismay sets in, and the person may seek another order of conformity or break down and rebel against the system, falling prey to another conventional system.

It is a huge problem when the church, by default, resorts to transforming people through the same methods. It turns our faith into a religion. We are selling a false gospel every time we try to fit believers into a mold. Bible study, Scripture memory, meditation, theological study, and formal education all churn out another "good Christian" or trained leader, but in themselves do not produce a transformed believer.

On the mission field, if I am offering the gospel packaged in a transformation-by-conformity parcel, I am just another religious zealot trying to win converts to a religion.

TRANSFORMATION THROUGH CREATION

The other kind of transformation is transformation through creation. God creates a new person, putting a clean heart in those who come to Jesus Christ. Romans 6–8 is all about this concept that works because of a new identity in Jesus Christ, not the other way around. Our identity is determined first through our unity with Christ, and it produces a reasonable outcome of holiness and righteousness. This dynamic of change starts with God, flows into the human spirit, wells up in a love that fills the mind and heart, and then breaks out in actions and words. It is *inspired!*

What makes the Christian faith unique is that it offers a real and permanent transformation. Religions provide ways to cope and fix symptoms of problems, but Jesus Christ gives us a new identity and brings us out into freedom; this is transformation by creation.

CHAPTER FIVE
TWO PROGRAMS OF TRANSFORMATION

The Bible teaches that all people who have ever existed belong to one of two families—the family of Satan or the family of God,[50] each named after its head. You've probably heard the beautiful message, "God loves you and has a plan for your life." But have you ever heard, "Satan hates you and has a plan for your life"? Both families, God's and Satan's, have ongoing "transformation programs" running for their members.

THE FDD

The apostle Paul describes Satan's transformation program in this way:

> *So this I say, and affirm together with the Lord, that you walk no longer just as the Gentiles also walk, in the futility of their mind, being darkened in their understanding, excluded from the life of God because of the ignorance that is in them, because of the hardness of their heart; and they, having become callous, have given themselves over to sensuality for the practice of every kind of impurity with greediness.*
> *— Ephesians 4:17–19 NASB 1995*

---

[50] Matthew 13:24–30, 36–43. The parable of the wheat and tares.

I appreciate how the New American Standard Bible translation makes clear the ongoing nature of the process. Notice it uses "being darkened" and "having become callous"; this is clearly about a continuous process of change, a transformation. In verse 20, Paul describes "the old self, which is being corrupted in accordance with the lusts of deceit." The text shows a progression that starts with a futile mind and leads to darkened understanding and, ultimately, separation from the life of God, which is death. Lust and deceit drive the process, which produces sensuality, impurity, and greed.

Figure 2. The FDD cycle of the old self

I call this the FDD cycle, which stands for Futility, Darkness, and Death. Satan's family is actively cranking out depravity through lust and greed in its members' lives, a fact that is important to keep in mind as we witness and interact with the world around us. FDD is Satan's plan for his family, and it is well entrenched in entertainment, news, politics, business, and family life in the world. It is everywhere, except in the presence of God.

THE HRC

In Ephesians 4, the apostle goes on to describe God's transformative plan for His family. I call it the Holiness–Righteousness Cycle (HRC).

> *But you did not learn Christ in this way, if indeed you have heard Him and have been taught in Him, just as truth is in Jesus, that, in reference to your former manner of life, you lay aside the old self, which is being corrupted in accordance with the lusts of deceit, and that you be renewed in the spirit of your mind, and put on the new self, which in the likeness of God has been created in righteousness and holiness of the truth.*
>
> *— Ephesians 4:20–24 NASB 1995*

God's transformative plan for our lives is for us to leave the old self, take it off like an old dirty coat, and put on the righteousness of Jesus Christ. The plan is that when we join the family of God, the Spirit of God comes to reside in us, bringing with Him the mind of Christ. Renewal from our newly created spirit spreads into our soul, where our thoughts form and our actions originate. At that point, we break out from the old family, leave it behind, and abandon its cycle of futility, darkness, and death. What was familiar and comfortable becomes the enemy; we can no longer stand the lust and deceit. The believer develops a deep hatred for sin, an allergic reaction to it, resulting in genuine mourning over it and repentance from it. On the flip side of forsaking the old family is clinging to the family of God. The deep disgust with sin comes with profound love and thirst for the righteousness of God. This disgust for sin and desire for righteousness is part and parcel of becoming a child of God.

The Ephesians 4 passage, in combination with Romans 6 through 8, forms the groundwork for my understanding of the transformation experience. I had to come to terms with the fact that there are two of me, one old and dead, the other created new in Christ. It seemed that in everything I did, I had to decide if I would act like my old self, a member of Satan's family, or as a member of the household of God. I learned to ask myself, *FDD or HRC?* Every time I chose FDD, I reaped severe consequences. Through my personal experience, I can attest to the truth of the saying "Be sure your sin will find you out." On the other hand, I have never regretted choosing the HRC, nor have I ever met or heard of someone who has.

A story my mother told me illustrates life with two identities. She was born in 1922, and her father died when she was around twelve years old. On the day he died, the family realized that they didn't photograph him, so they decided to take one before his burial. They had to prop him up in a sitting position and take the picture, but naturally, the body was not cooperating. They had my mother, who was small enough to hide, crouch behind the body and hold it up with her back. She said they combed the hair and shaved some facial hair to make it look good. Ewww. Can you imagine messing around with a dead body trying to make it look good? And then holding it up as if it were alive? Yet this is what we do every day as believers when we take out our old dead self and pet it, comb its hair, talk to it, and prop it up to make it look alive. It's what we are doing when we choose to live in the old self, acting and behaving according to a futile mind, darkened understanding, and death. Many who profess faith in Jesus Christ still cling to the old self, dragging it around like a corpse everywhere they go.

In summary, there are two families and two systems of transformation, and both produce behavior and actions. The decision to put on the righteousness of Jesus Christ in a given situation is at the very root of transformation. In this framework, the liberating power of the gospel of Jesus Christ gives us the ability to choose God's way over Satan's. It happens in a moment; it overflows from the Spirit of God into the human spirit, moves outward into the believer's heart and soul, and results in action.

CHAPTER SIX
MOMENTS OF DECISION

A transformed life is a harvest we reap that was sown in individual decisions to obey God. Stephen Covey laid out a sequence that shows the connection between our thoughts and our destiny. He said, "Sow a thought, reap an action; sow an action, reap a habit; sow a habit, reap a character; sow a character, reap a destiny."[51] It is a thoroughly biblical concept and an excellent insight into what shapes our character and destiny. The point here is that our thoughts ultimately shape us. Therefore, if I want to change my life, I must start with my thoughts.

Proverbs 4:23 says, "Guard your heart above all else, for it determines the course of your life." And Romans 12:2 says, "Don't copy the behavior and customs of this world, but let God transform you into a new person by changing the way you think." These verses tell us that transformation happens in the heart, which is the seat of the mind, will, and emotion. It is a private place, hidden from the sight of people—but not from God.

In studying the phrase "be transformed" in Romans 12:2, we find it is in the passive voice, meaning we allow ourselves to be transformed. Paul is urging us to surrender to the Holy Spirit, like a patient who submits their body to a surgeon. When the decision to surrender to the Holy Spirit becomes a habit, we grow into the likeness of Jesus Christ.

[51] Covey, Stephen R. The Seven Habits of Highly Effective People: Powerful Lessons in Personal Change. New York, NY: Simon and Schuster, 1989.

Here is how the apostle Paul explains the origin of a transformed life:

> *Those who are dominated by the sinful nature think about sinful things, but those who are controlled by the Holy Spirit think about things that please the Spirit. So letting your sinful nature control your mind leads to death. But letting the Spirit control your mind leads to life and peace. For the sinful nature is always hostile to God. It never did obey God's laws, and it never will. That's why those who are still under the control of their sinful nature can never please God.*
>
> *But you are not controlled by your sinful nature. You are controlled by the Spirit if you have the Spirit of God living in you. (And remember that those who do not have the Spirit of Christ living in them do not belong to him at all.) And Christ lives within you, so even though your body will die because of sin, the Spirit gives you life because you have been made right with God. The Spirit of God, who raised Jesus from the dead, lives in you. And just as God raised Christ Jesus from the dead, he will give life to your mortal bodies by this same Spirit living within you. — Romans 8:5–11*

The Holy Spirit, who resides in the believer, gives life and communicates with our spirit the desires of God. We then choose either to submit to Him or rebel; it is a *moment of decision*. These moments combine to determine whether we transform into the likeness of Jesus Christ or that of the world. Every time we submit to God, we take a step forward toward His image, and every time we rebel, we take a step away. You may have heard the saying "you are who you worship";[52] this process spells it out for us. Until the Holy Spirit aligns your heart with God's, you won't be able to engage in these moments of decision. Given that transformation is a function of choosing God in moments of decision, we must find out how we can consistently make the right choice. What factors are involved, and how can we improve our decisions favorably for transformation?

---

[52] Psalm 115:8.

THE HOLY SPIRIT

The Holy Spirit is God, and He is the primary mover in the moment of decision. The Bible teaches that there is one God in three Persons: Father, Son, and Holy Spirit. You have heard the good news that Jesus died on the cross, taking your death penalty in your place and that He rose from the dead on the third day. That event, which took place two thousand years ago, is what God did to save those who are His own. Transformation begins with coming to Jesus Christ through belief in His sacrifice on the cross and His resurrection.

The Holy Spirit mediates this step, and He places the faith and the desire in you to belong to Him. When we choose to connect with God through faith in Jesus Christ, His Holy Spirit will come and live in us, side by side with our spirit. He will renew our spirit through the same power that raised Jesus from the dead, and we will then be able to relate to God. We won't be able to relate to Him until our spirit is made new.

In his letter to the Ephesians, the apostle Paul says to the believers, "And now you Gentiles have also heard the truth, the Good News that God saves you. And when you believed in Christ, he identified you as his own by giving you the Holy Spirit, whom he promised long ago" (Ephesians 1:13). To the Corinthian believers, he said, "Don't you realize that all of you together are the temple of God and that the Spirit of God lives in you?" (1 Corinthians 3:16).

The Holy Spirit is the initiator of faith and the driver of transformation, which He will complete in us.

> So you have not received a spirit that makes you fearful slaves. Instead, you received God's Spirit when he adopted you as his own children. Now we call him, "Abba, Father." For his Spirit joins with our spirit to affirm that we are God's children. And since we are his children, we are his heirs. In fact, together with Christ we are heirs of God's glory. But if we are to share his glory, we must also share his suffering.
> — Romans 8:15–17

> For we know that when this earthly tent we live in is taken down (that is, when we die and leave this earthly body), we

will have a house in heaven, an eternal body made for us by God himself and not by human hands. We grow weary in our present bodies, and we long to put on our heavenly bodies like new clothing. For we will put on heavenly bodies; we will not be spirits without bodies. While we live in these earthly bodies, we groan and sigh, but it's not that we want to die and get rid of these bodies that clothe us. Rather, we want to put on our new bodies so that these dying bodies will be swallowed up by life. God himself has prepared us for this, and as a guarantee he has given us his Holy Spirit.
— 2 Corinthians 5:1–5

In addition to His role as initiator and guarantor, the Holy Spirit also supplies the fuel for transformation. This strength comes through to the believer's spirit in the form of love, joy, peace, patience, kindness, goodness, faithfulness, gentleness, and self-control.[53]

This help from the Holy Spirit is necessary; without it, we cannot choose obedience to God in moments of decision. He doesn't take away our freedom to choose, but He is there to help us recognize the right choice.

So, what can we do to make use of His help in the moment of decision? Here is one crucial answer: be filled with the Holy Spirit. Ephesians 5 tells us how to be filled with the Spirit:

Don't be drunk with wine, because that will ruin your life. Instead, be filled with the Holy Spirit, singing psalms and hymns and spiritual songs among yourselves, and making music to the Lord in your hearts. And give thanks for everything to God the Father in the name of our Lord Jesus Christ. And further, submit to one another out of reverence for Christ. — Ephesians 5:18–21

Some may have the impression that the filling of the Spirit is a state of mystical power and creepy behavior. But the Ephesians 5 passage is not so hard to understand. It commands us to be filled, which means that it

---

[53] Galatians 5:22,23.

is something within reach of every believer. It also prescribes three things for us to do:

1. Worship God individually and corporately.
2. In everything, give thanks to God the Father in the name of Jesus Christ.
3. Submit to one another out of reverence for Christ.

There is an implicit but crucial component of this command. It is that we need one another to fulfill it. Corporate worship, for instance, requires the participation of a group. And the third command is startling. What does submission to one another have to do with being filled with the Holy Spirit? We'll explore the relationship between the two in the next chapter.

THE WORD OF GOD

In a moment of decision, the Holy Spirit uses the Word of God to speak truth into our lives. Paul teaches us that "all Scripture is inspired by God and is useful to teach us what is true and to make us realize what is wrong in our lives. It corrects us when we are wrong and teaches us to do what is right. God uses it to prepare and equip his people to do every good work" (2 Timothy 3:16–17). And John records Jesus's prayer to the Father, "Make them holy by your truth; teach them your word, which is truth" (John 17:17).

The Bible is the Word of God, a set of sixty-six books and letters written thousands of years ago. They were written over a period of roughly 1,600 years, from 1500 B.C. to around 92 A.D., by forty different authors, each inspired under the guidance of the Holy Spirit of God.[54] God's thoughts were recorded by these authors, which is why the Bible is called the Word of God. The Word of God transforms our lives when we take it into our hearts.

As created beings, we are unable to produce a single original thought. We can associate ideas and recombine them to discover new concepts, but we cannot create them. Artists observe life and nature and represent

---

[54] 2 Peter 1:20,21.

them. It is the same for engineers, scientists, philosophers, and every other human intellect. They all have to perceive first, then assimilate and associate, and then produce. What we mean when we say that we are inspired is that something outside of us forms an impression in our minds that causes us to think, but the thought does not originate within us—it comes from outside. All creation, including Satan, shares this inability to create thought; created beings can only perceive what God created and reformulate it. God is the creator of all things.

This fact about created beings means that the Truth is not within us; it is external, and it must come by revelation, which passes through our perception and enters our mind. This channel from the world to our minds consists of our five senses and our spirit, forming a filter. It is why none of us can claim to have the Absolute Truth; what we have is filtered truth, with a small *t*. Unlike what we possess, the Word of God is the Absolute Truth, a solid reference point, an anchor in a sea of differing perceptions. It is God's revelation to us, and it is trustworthy. In a moment of decision, it is indispensable if we are to make the right choice.

Once the Holy Spirit is living in us, exposure to the Word of God activates the powerful agents of transformation. Through them, God communicates with us and reveals Himself.

In a moment of decision, we need to have the Word of God present in our hearts. In the summer of 1983, a few weeks after I came to Jesus Christ, I enrolled in a Navigators Summer Training Program in Syracuse, NY. It was a great experience that laid the groundwork for my spiritual formation. In one of the sessions, a speaker shared with us the Hand Illustration to explain how we can take in the Word of God. He said that we use our hands to grasp and manipulate objects. The fingers work together with the palm to give us the fantastic ability to hold things, write, draw, and perform precise tasks that require extreme skill. The fingers and their roles compare to five different ways we take in the Word of God.

The pinky is the weakest of the fingers, and it represents hearing the Word of God. The ring finger is a little sturdier, and it represents reading the Word. The middle finger is more robust, and it represents studying the Word. Finally, the index finger, which is the strongest and most dexterous, represents memorizing the Word. After our speaker made the index finger comparison, he took his Bible and tried to hold it with the pinky alone, then with two or more fingers, but he couldn't grab it. He managed to get a hold of it with the four digits, but it wasn't a very firm grip. He then held out his hand and showed how the thumb juxtaposes each of the other fingers. God designed the hand with a thumb, the strongest of all digits, to work as a vice grip for the other fingers. He said the thumb represents meditation on the Word of God. Each of the fingers is functional when used with the thumb. When all four digits are on one side, and the thumb is on the other, the grip is formidable. His point was that we should hear, read, study, and memorize the Word of God, all the while sealing the Word in our hearts by meditating on it.

Several years later, I took a course called Teaching to Change Lives. The professor gave a memorable illustration of what it means to meditate. He said meditation is like popping a piece of candy into your mouth; you hold it against your palate with your tongue, then flip it over to the side and move it around to another part of your mouth. As you do, the flavor spreads, and you taste it all over. As it melts in your mouth, you swallow the juices a little at a time. Meditation on the Word of God is the same. Take a word or sentence from the Bible, pop it in your mind, then turn it over, looking at it from different perspectives. Ask what, where, when, who, how, and why.

The Word of God is a treasure, a gift from God to reveal His nature, character, and will—thoughts that are most worthy of occupying our hearts and souls. As we meditate on His Word, His thoughts permeate our minds and impart life to us. In a moment of decision, it is critical to have His thoughts in our hearts.[55]

From 1999 to 2017, Sandy and I led the Access Team, a ministry team made up of several families. We met weekly to pray and plan, and these were extraordinary meetings that we remember fondly. In 2012, we started a K–12 school named Access International School in Aley, Lebanon.

For our school logo, I chose a tree with twelve leaves; near the root, written in tiny letters on the trunk, were the words "Psalm 1." This is one of my own life verses. I decided on that passage of Scripture as the school's theme verse because it contains the most incredible promise in the Word of God. See if you can find the guarantee:

---

[55] 1 Corinthians 2:13–16.

Oh, the joys of those who do not follow the advice of the wicked,
or stand around with sinners, or join in with mockers.

But they delight in the law of the Lord,
meditating on it day and night.

They are like trees planted along the riverbank,
bearing fruit each season.

Their leaves never wither,
and they prosper in all they do.

But not the wicked!
They are like worthless chaff, scattered by the wind.

They will be condemned at the time of judgment.
Sinners will have no place among the godly.

For the Lord watches over the path of the godly,
but the path of the wicked leads to destruction.

— Psalm 1:1–6

This psalm tells us that if we meditate on the Word of God continually and abide in it like a tree rooted by a river, we will prosper in everything we do! Isn't this an incredible guarantee? What is even more remarkable is that history bears witness that it is true. It is a tested and proven fact the Lord teaches us; if we meditate, absorb, and live according to His instructions, we will succeed in *everything* we do.

The Bible is God's revelation to all humanity, not only Christians. Neither culture nor religion can restrain it or make it off-limits for anyone. But as the general director of the school, I had to get the licensing and permits from the Lebanese authorities. One of the licenses was from the Ministry of Commerce for the copyright of our school logo. I sent our application with a sample logo, asking that they register it as belonging to our school. A few days later, I received a phone call from a lady at the ministry. She asked me if I realized that the logo had the inscription "Psalm

1" on the tree trunk, corresponding to a passage from the Old Testament. From my family name, she could tell that I am not from a Christian family and was so puzzled by the quoted verse that she felt the need to call and warn me. I told her I was aware of it and included the biblical reference on the logo because it speaks of the most significant promise ever given to humanity. She replied with, "More power to you!" Like her, many who come to our school for the first time are shocked to find out we teach the Bible to our students. But they do not object once they realize that we are using it not to push a religion but to show who God is.

Many people ask the question, "Why do you teach the Bible at your school?"[56] It is because the Bible reveals God, who is the Creator of the universe and all that is in it. He is also the giver of life, and there is no life apart from Him. When students study the revelation of God, they can understand themselves, the world around them, and their place in it. This understanding enables them to reach their full potential by being transformed into the people that God intends them to be.

Here are some things to consider regarding the Bible:

- The Bible relates all knowledge to God, the origin of all things. This fact alone provides a context in which to place new information that we learn.
- The Bible provides a way for us to love God, ourselves, and others. It becomes the foundation on which we build our classroom instruction.
- The Bible shows us that God loves us, and we need love, all of us. His love fills the emptiness in our hearts, and we want it to fill the hearts of our students.
- The Bible shows us the meaning of life and prepares us for eternity. It helps us set our life goals in a way that considers all seasons of life, even preparing us for death.
- The Bible transforms our hearts and minds and defends us against sin and immorality, weapons that destroy many lives. Pornography and drug abuse are ravaging our youth, and we need to teach them how to deal with these deadly habits. The Bible does that as it equips us for a life of godliness.

---

[56] The answer is published on the FAQ page of our website, www.access.edu.lb.

THE PEOPLE OF GOD

The Holy Spirit and the Word of God are present in the place where moments of decision take place. A third participant in our moments of decision is our fellow people of God. In a moment of decision, we need the support of a Christian community.

> *Two people are better off than one, for they can help each other succeed. If one person falls, the other can reach out and help. But someone who falls alone is in real trouble. Likewise, two people lying close together can keep each other warm. But how can one be warm alone? A person standing alone can be attacked and defeated, but two can stand back-to-back and conquer. Three are even better, for a triple-braided cord is not easily broken. — Ecclesiastes 4:9–12*

As mentioned earlier, the moment of decision takes place in the believer's heart, hidden from others but visible to God. When the believer allows one or more trustworthy people into this private place, the additional support helps draw him or her closer to God. We all need help making decisions, and rebelling in secret is a lot easier than rebelling in public. A group of godly people provides us with protection from deceit and temptation.

In 2015, I built a barn in my orchard and used it to house five milking goats and six sheep. I started the project to learn about sustainable farming for an experience I might use to help start farms throughout the region. Such farms provide a steady income to families, all members share the workload, and they don't require advanced education. There was another, more personal reason for the barn; I like taking care of sheep and goats.

I learned that our sheep and goats each have their own personalities and attitudes. But when they are in a crowd, they act very differently than when they are alone. The flock is a strong influence that sweeps them all. Our orchard has about 250 feet of road frontage and the sheep-like to assemble by the fence to watch cars and pedestrians. They'll graze peacefully and lift their heads now and then to see what's coming down the road. One day, they were startled by an approaching rhythmic thud. It was the stomping of boots of a company of a hundred soldiers on their exercise run passing by our orchard. When the troop reached our grove, the sheep lined up inside the fence parallel to them and joined the procession. They blended into the rhythmic beat and stuck beside the crowd. As the soldiers ran, the sheep trotted along to the end of the orchard boundary and would have continued if not for the fence. That was a funny scene, and I wish I had captured it on video. It reminds me of the power of groups as it applies to people as well; we get swept by groups, and we feel a pull to do as they do. If you have ever had to stand in opposition to a large group, you realize its power, and it takes real determination to overcome the tug inside to go along.

Figure 3. Gathered by the fence.

Get on the bandwagon! Join the crowd! Humans are naturally prone to answering this call, yet person by person, we seem to believe we're an exception. We have the sense that we are independent individuals in control of our personal choices and destinies. The reality is that we live and behave in communities, heavily influenced by group dynamics. We see the group influence used consistently in marketing, politics, and social interactions. The option is not whether we should join the crowd or not, but which group we will join.

A question we should ask is whether transforming relationships occur exclusively between believers. The answer is yes. The kind of relationship I am presenting here is revealed in the Bible between believers in Jesus Christ only. If a believer has a deep-level relationship with a non-believer, such as a spouse, God can still use the dynamics of the connection to transform the believer and bring the non-believer to faith in Jesus Christ. But this is quite different from the transforming relationship described here, in which all members can enter into the presence of God together to worship and discern His leading. It is also different in that the non-believer is actively enrolled in the FDD (futility, darkness, and death) cycle of depravity and has no way to choose God in moments of decision. A believing spouse with a strong network of believers around him or her can benefit from transforming relationships, but an unbelieving spouse won't be able to participate.

CHAPTER SEVEN

TRANSFORMING RELATIONSHIPS

We are building our understanding of transforming relationships one brick at a time. We began by defining transformation by the gospel of Jesus Christ in contrast to other kinds of transformation. We then showed from the Bible that transformation by the gospel of Jesus could come about only through God's holiness and righteousness program, as explained in Ephesians 4. Upon that concept, we added the insight that transformation results from the choices we make in many moments of decision. Now we are adding the next brick of truth: God wants us to be in a web of relationships that transform us.

Building relationships that transform is not a coincidence. The intent required to form these relationships motivated us to design a residential training program to spend extended time developing long-term relationships with potential leaders. While week-long conferences are excellent leadership training opportunities, they don't allow the time necessary to know the trainees and grow with them.

A typical leadership candidate would have been to several training conferences and showed good leadership qualities. They usually came to us through referral by partners in the region. Finishing the program would mean continued financial support until they are established in their ministry. In some cases, as we interacted more closely with the candidate, we started to develop concerns. Regular interaction with them uncovered some family or personal dynamics that had remained secret for years. Although they had completed several Bible study series in their home country, attended conferences, and participated in other training programs, their secret life had gone undetected. In extreme cases, we had to ask them to leave the training program because they continued their bad habits. If it hadn't been for the extended time with them, we would have never discovered their secret life and would have designated and supported them as leaders in their community.

Other people who spent extended time with our team at Access are now active and fruitful leaders in their communities. Some stayed for as long as five years with us. During their time at Access, they experienced inner healing, life in a servant community, and transforming relationships. Although it is a prolonged process, residential leadership training has produced some excellent results for many. It has broadened their vision and understanding of who God is and what He is doing in the world.

The residential leadership training at Access took a lot of determination and intent to get started; it developed over several years. The Access Team firmly believed that transformation takes place in a community of believers in Jesus Christ over time, life on life. It goes beyond the one-on-one discipleship model by engaging the whole person, not only their intellect.

Residential leadership training was and remains our standard practice for training leaders in ministry. This process of transformation requires physical presence with each other and a common task to accomplish. It also requires trust among the community to be transparent with at least a few other members.

Large organizations usually don't have time for extended incarnational training. They are interested in developing standardized programs that are short, predictable, and reproducible. Many forces drive the demand for such training programs. Agencies build their strategy to plant a certain number of churches or reach a certain number of people groups by a given deadline. Time is of the essence, so the shorter the program, the better. Another benefit is that these training programs offer measurable results that are easy to convey to potential donors, enhancing the ability to raise funds for the mission. Many church leaders are eager to teach conferences because this matches their gifting; it is an easy and clean way for them to be involved in cross-cultural ministry. The expert flies into the country for a week, shares his or her teaching, and heads back home. The trend among missionary organizations working in the Middle East, and perhaps other regions, is to improvise these quick injections of leadership training in conferences that last a few days.

I have participated in such conferences, both as a trainee and as a trainer, for two decades. They are of great benefit to many, but they fall short of being transformative. We have discovered that people can sit through the best biblical teaching and sing worship to God yet return to their inactive lifestyles at home. They manage to hide in public during conferences, obscuring their abuse, anger, pride, and deceit.

Many books and sermons extol the benefits of listening as a way to love others, and indeed we ought to learn to be good listeners. But the listening that takes place at church and leadership conferences often has far too narrow a scope. When the church meets, we spend most of our time listening to one or two people, and then we return home to wrestle alone with personal strongholds that haunt us. We need time for a different sort of listening when the church meets: each member should have an opportunity to tell his or her story, and others should respond with an affirmation or reproof as the situation requires. I'm not saying we should tell all our secrets to everyone assembled, but someone trustworthy and competent should know what is going on in our lives, and they should have access to speak the truth to us.

I am highly critical of many of our modern approaches to training conferences and church services, and I disagree with how many ministries today operate. Every time I share these views, I get a lot of pushback from mission leaders—and leaders from the US in particular. But I firmly believe that we, the Church, are shirking our responsibility to foster transformative relationships among believers. As church leaders, we must intentionally seek to know the people in our care and help them build healthy relationships with others. The big meetings are good, and we should keep them, but they should not be the main event; far more crucial are the small webs of transforming relationships.

In 2006, I joined several leaders from the US and the Middle East in forming a partnership. One of the association's goals was to plan and design leadership training programs for believers in the Middle East. The association put me in charge of leadership training alongside the lead pastor of a large congregation in the US. At our first leadership planning meeting, we prayed, and then the pastor began by outlining what he wanted me to do. He said, "Okay, you'll take charge of gathering as many trainees as you can, and we'll schedule a conference time and venue, then I'll fly in and train them in leadership." That was our first and last meeting.

In the meeting, I pointed out to my partner in ministry that he was making many assumptions. One was that the best way to train people was to teach them directly. Seminaries train preachers and teachers to teach, so teaching has become the most emphasized and exercised gift in the Church today. Teaching is a thoroughly biblical mandate, and I have nothing against it. But teaching alone is not what God has prescribed for us. Ephesians 4 outlines several offices in the Church: apostles, prophets, evangelists, preachers, and teachers. These are roles that should be present in churches, but only rarely do we see them expressed.

Teaching alone is like a craftsman with one tool in his or her box. Or like a car with an engine and nothing else. I recently learned that all plants require seventeen elements to thrive. The roots absorb these inorganic molecules—all they need to live and bear fruit. The least available element limits a plant's ability to bear fruit. This limitation means we can load the soil with nitrogen, but if the plant doesn't have enough boron or copper, or manganese, it will not bear good fruit. It is the same with transformation; many factors work together to complete this work in us. One of these is teaching, but it is not the only one.

Teaching has become the Church's go-to, default activity, and we don't question its usefulness no matter the context. The imbalance gives us a false sense of accomplishment before we've reached the goal of transformation. Hearing a message is very important, but it is only a tiny part of the big picture of training leaders.

The second assumption my partner made was that the leadership concepts he taught in the US were what believers in the Middle East needed. But he failed to consider the cultural differences between these groups of believers. The pressing concerns of the church in the Middle East include issues like persecution and poverty. And believers in the US and the Middle East live within different societal constructs. Most US pastors' sermons address the individual, not a community, but this does not fit the Middle Eastern context.

Americans assume that all individuals should make their own decisions, while Middle Eastern communities seek consensus. In western societies, the family consists of a father, mother, and their children. In the Middle East, a family includes grandparents, grandchildren, aunts, uncles, and cousins. Also, the Arab–Israeli conflict is a stumbling block for many, and any leadership training program should address it from a thoroughly biblical perspective. This topic is not an easy one to handle.

Our partnership in charting a course for leadership training ended abruptly. The pastor could not believe I objected to his approach. He said that he had trained many leaders at seminaries, teaching as many as three hundred students at a time. How could I have the audacity to say his methods were not valid? I clarified that I thought it had some validity, especially in the US, but it was not sufficient. The clarification did not help; my partner was offended by that time, and he was not open to my input.

Thankfully to God, that story didn't end there. Several years later, the same pastor came to visit me at Access, and he told me that what I said back in 2006 hurt his feelings. He also asked me to forgive him for his response, which was prideful. In turn, I asked his forgiveness for my harsh words that hurt his feelings, and we sensed the peace of Jesus Christ restoring our fellowship.

My conflict with this pastor summarizes well my experience with other leaders of large organizations. They believe that their high attendance numbers validate their methods, and they use their platform to tell others how to mimic what they do. Numbers in attendance or the number of followers on a social media account are the ways that the world measures success, not the way God measures it. He looks at the heart. The number of people transformed into the likeness of Jesus Christ is a better indicator of ministry success, and we cannot take credit for it; it is the work of the Holy Spirit.

Many churches in the US seek to become large congregations with big budgets and campuses. I don't write off these ministries, and I believe that God is in many of them. But they are only one step in the right direction; we must do more to continue on the path toward transformation. Church growth strategies are in high demand, and elder boards seem occupied with risk management and growth. Most seem unwilling to risk what they think they have achieved to make the necessary changes to form transforming relationships in their congregations. But God will have His way, one way or another. The recent COVID-19 lockdown effectively stripped congregations of the ability to meet. Multimillion-dollar complexes were empty, waiting for the Sunday crowds to return. It is impossible from this vantage point to predict what long-term changes will result from this sudden disruption. But once we benefit from hindsight, I hope we find that we used this opportunity to reevaluate our goals and methods and didn't merely rush back to "business as normal" as soon as ordinances allowed it.

I recognize that my comments on current practices in discipleship and leadership development have been quite critical. What I have shown in this book so far, to no small degree, is an integration of concepts published in many articles and books on discipleship and transformed lives. I have studied and memorized passages of God's Word and experienced these issues firsthand as a minister of the gospel of Jesus Christ. It is my perspective, and I hope it offers new insights and practical advice on transformation. But I don't want to provide only criticism; I want to present an alternative as well.

Our current models of discipleship and leadership training are based almost exclusively on the attributes of the individual. They don't consider relationship dynamics, yet relationships are at least half of the equation. When it comes to the role of relationships in transformation, I will present some ideas that I haven't seen spelled out in Christian literature. The central thesis of this book is that transformation happens in a specific kind of connection, which I call transforming relationships. I am not discounting the importance of character as part of the process. Still, Christian literature has so far ignored the influence of relational dynamics on group behavior, which is why I want to place a particular focus on it here.

The phrase "transforming relationships" can be used in two ways. If "transforming" is a verb and "relationships" is the object, then the sentence describes the transformation of relationships. In this case, it's a how-to statement. Alternatively, if the word "transforming" is an adjective, it refers to a type of relationship that transforms people or organizations. I intend to retain this double meaning. I want to talk about the characteristics of relationships that change others, and I want to talk about transforming shallow relationships into change-bringing systems.

In the Appendix on Complexity Theory, one of the four concepts presented is that network diagrams are useful in representing complex systems. These diagrams connect circles or other geometric shapes by lines to show the components of a given system and their configuration. A circle denotes an entity, sometimes called *actor* or *node* in network analysis literature, and a line represents a relationship, called *tie* or *link*. An actor can be a person, a country, a company, or an entity in a complex system. The field of Network Analysis studies the dynamics of interactions between actors and ties. It can help communicate profound phenomena of complex systems, like centrality, modularity, structural equivalence, diffusion of innovation, and more.[57]

We don't need to delve deeper into Network Theory; I want to point out that there are two categories of dynamics in a network that drive the system: the actors' attributes and the ties' properties. These two categories are not isolated from each other; they work together to produce behavior. In this book, I am focusing on the attributes of actors and the properties of ties that make them transformational. Following is an alternative model of discipleship and leadership development that outlines five characteristics of transforming relationships.

OUR CENTER

We have explored the two systems of transformation, the FDD and the HRC, and showed how our actions are rooted in moments of decision. Now it is time to combine these biblical truths, using Network Analysis lingo, to investigate relationships that transform us into the likeness of Jesus Christ. Forming this kind of network of relationships is the first step toward a community of transformed believers.

I have produced three network diagrams to illustrate the contrast of ways we relate to those around us. One of the sketches is a configuration with relationships that we consider typical in the world. The other shows relationships that transform us into the likeness of Jesus Christ.

---

[57] Wasserman, Stanley and Katherine Faust. 1994. Social Network Analysis: Methods and Applications. Cambridge; NY: Cambridge University Press.

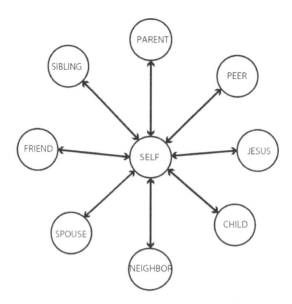

Figure 4. Representation of a Typical Believer's Web of Relationships.

The first diagram is a representation of a believer in Jesus Christ who has friends and family ties. These ties can be strong or weak, positive or negative, depending on the quality of the relationship between the two members. The arrow indicates the direction of flow in the tie. These ties have arrows in both directions, a "give and take" type of connection. Every actor in the network is labeled based on their tie to SELF, so naturally, it is at the center. In this view, the role of each actor in the life of SELF determines their position.

This self-centered web is considered normal for humans, but there is a problem with it. If we perceive ourselves as the center of our universe, then the rest of creation is merely a context for our own experience of life. In our natural selves, we evaluate people's worth and objects by how they reflect on us.

Sandy and I got engaged to be married in 1986, and a couple at our church recommended that we read a book entitled *The Mystery of Marriage* by Mike Mason.[58] It remains to this day the best biblical discourse I

---

[58] Mike Mason, The Mystery of Marriage, Doubleday Religious Publishing Group, 2001, accessed June 8, 2020, retrieved from books.google.com/books/about/The_Mystery_of_ Marriage. html?id=eO8zPQAACAAJ.

have read on the marriage relationship. In chapter 1, Mason talks about Otherness. I thought the word otherness was strange, but it does describe the state of our soul very well. In my own words, I gleaned from that chapter that we don't honestly believe that there are others out there besides ourselves. We see people and things as props intended for our benefit; they exist to provide context and meaning for our experience. In the self-centered web, we are at the center of the universe, and everything else revolves around us, so we evaluate and treat others from that perspective. Mason says that God intends marriage to jolt us out of this self-centered state and make us aware that we are one of many others.

You may be thinking I am too hard on humanity in this indictment, but this is what the Bible teaches, and I have experienced that it's true. When Adam rebelled against God, the sinful nature entered and festered deep in the human soul. It corrupted God's original design so radically that our most honorable and generous deeds are nothing more than efforts to please ourselves. We look on the outside and evaluate actions by what is visible, but God looks at the heart and sees the source. He considers our motives as well as our actions.

In the Gospel of Luke, Jesus makes a shocking statement:

> *A large crowd was following Jesus. He turned around and said to them, "If you want to be my disciple, you must, by comparison, hate everyone else—your father and mother, wife and children, brothers and sisters—yes, even your own life.*
>
> *Otherwise, you cannot be my disciple. And if you do not carry your own cross and follow me, you cannot be my disciple."*
> *— Luke 14:25–27*

Can you believe it? Jesus made it a requirement that we hate everyone else and ourselves if we want to be His disciples. This passage requires some explanation, which is why the New Living Translation inserts the qualifier "in comparison" to emphasize that He wants our relationship with Him to be first and foremost. But I think there is more to it than a comparison of the intensity of the connections; He is talking about a different kind of relationship.

In the self-centered web, we use our resources and capabilities to relate to others. We love our family with human love, which is quite different from the love of God. In the best possible case, we negotiate relationships based on mutual benefit: "You scratch my back, and I'll scratch yours." The problem with such an agreement is that it is only as good as the two parties that make it. Note that it is an agreement between two parties.

Jesus is proposing a different kind of arrangement. It begins with an unbreakable connection to Him, followed by breaking the old links with everyone else—including self. He says we must deny ourselves and take up our cross daily and follow Him. The work of Jesus Christ on the cross is what makes it possible for us to connect with Him in a personal and eternal relationship. Paul summarizes this process well:

> *So we have stopped evaluating others from a human point of view. At one time we thought of Christ merely from a human point of view. How differently we know him now! This means that anyone who belongs to Christ has become a new person. The old life is gone; a new life has begun!*
> *— 2 Corinthians 5:16–17*

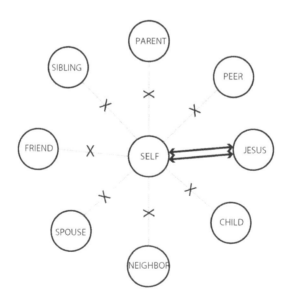

Figure 5. Luke 14:25–27 Transformation.

Once we enter this new life with Jesus Christ, we will relate to others through Him and His perspective. So when He commands us to love the Lord our God with all our mind, soul, spirit, and strength, and to love others like ourselves, we can obey. He is saying, "Stop loving yourself and others with your means; die to yourself and use My love."

When I came to Christ, I gained the capacity to see others through God's perspective, and it has become the basis of my new relationships. I had to completely dispose of my old connections with my mother and my siblings and start relating to them through Jesus Christ. As my ties shifted, Christ replaced *self* as the center. I believe this is the whole point of the Luke 14 passage. Jesus wants to be the center around which our lives and relations form.

The first shift from natural to transforming relationships is to establish Jesus at their center. Such a change takes place when we confess Jesus Christ as our Lord before others. One way or another, new believers need to identify as people who belong to Jesus Christ and commit to reestablishing relationships according to His guidance and desires. As we enter new relationships, we must proclaim our first allegiance to Jesus Christ.

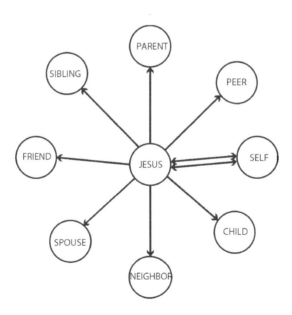

Figure 6. Representation of the Kingdom of God Web of Relationships.

In Luke's Gospel, Jesus uses the term "Kingdom of God" to describe what it is like to be related to God. He makes specific contrasts between the way we do things in the world and how it is in the Kingdom of God. His teaching addresses our relationship with Him as individuals and as a community. It also addresses our relationships with fellow believers and with other people in general. In the next few sections, I want to explore His teaching to form a consistent set of characteristics of transforming relationships.

The first characteristic of a transforming relationship is that Jesus is at its center. The smallest Kingdom of God web you can form contains three actors: Jesus, yourself, and one other believer. How many do you suppose is the maximum number of actors that can be in such a web?

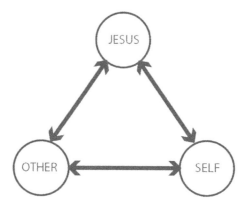

Figure 7. Model of a Transforming Relationship.

Once we have gone through the characteristics of the transforming relationship, it'll be evident that we can't have that kind of connection with every other believer; we have to select a few, only as many as we can relate to at a deep level.

I have experienced this type of relationship on the Access ministry team. We started the team in 1999 with one other family, and more joined later. Our vision for the team was to be united no matter what, accept each other's strengths and weaknesses and not allow them to form a wedge between us. We intentionally spelled out our commitment to Jesus

Christ and, because of Him, to one another. We were inspired to start this relationship because we got along well and were able to communicate freely. But it lasted and developed into a transforming relationship because Jesus was at its center. He was the reason for our unity and service on the team. The Access Team developed through stages. First, the focus was on unity. We weren't required to conform to one opinion in all matters, but we needed to be able to agree. Then, while making every effort to keep unity, God led us through a process of embracing diversity. We accepted the differences between us, and there were many. We had different cultures, personalities, gifting, and opinions. God helped us embrace these differences and use them for the benefit of the team. The two stages of finding unity and embracing diversity within our group took years to establish. After about seven years of working together, we sensed that God had given us the ability to discern spiritual matters together. It was not a mystical exercise, but the gain of a clear vision of what God is doing in the world around us; we found that we could see current events in the context of history and the Word of God.

Our experience on the Access Team changed our lives, thanks to what Jesus was doing through our relationships. They became a center of transformation not only for the team members but for the community in general. I will write more about the spread of transformation in *Transforming Community,* a companion book.

A SERVANT ROLE

The second characteristic of a transforming relationship is that those who enter into it assume the role of servants of Jesus Christ. The Bible clearly defines the role of any human as that of a servant. He created us to be servants, so we don't have a choice; we must serve someone or something. The choice we do have is whom to serve. The Bible narrows it down to two options, either God or the world.

Many Scripture passages talk about servanthood, but this particular passage shows how being human goes hand in hand with being a servant.

Don't be selfish; don't try to impress others. Be humble, thinking of others as better than yourselves. Don't look out only for your own interests, but take an interest in others, too.

You must have the same attitude that Christ Jesus had.

*Though he was God,
he did not think of equality with God as something to cling to.*

Instead, he gave up his divine privileges; he took the humble position of a slave and was born as a human being.

*When he appeared in human form,
he humbled himself in obedience to God and died a criminal's death on a cross. — Philippians 2:3–8*

Even when God Himself took on a human body, He became a servant. The passage is saying that becoming a human is to become a servant.

Jesus Christ, the center and head of every transforming relationship, is the pattern for us to imitate. He doesn't force us to conform; instead, He inspires us to walk as servants.

People in a web of transforming relationships function as servants of Jesus Christ. They perform acts of service for one another, but only because they are servants of Jesus first. Being a servant in a relationship with God means we obey Him as Jesus did and follow His plan for our lives. We submit to Him. To serve others in a transforming relationship, we cannot be selfish; we are not in it to impress, so we must be humble and put others in the relationship ahead of ourselves. Luke 17 provides a good description of how God thinks we should relate to each other in the Kingdom of God. A Kingdom of God relationship is another term for a transforming relationship.

One day Jesus said to his disciples, "There will always be temptations to sin, but what sorrow awaits the person who does the tempting! It would be better to be thrown into the sea with a millstone hung around your neck than to cause one of these little ones to fall into sin. So watch yourselves!

"If another believer sins, rebuke that person; then if there is repentance, forgive. Even if that person wrongs you seven times a day and each time turns again and asks forgiveness, you must forgive."

The apostles said to the Lord, "Show us how to increase our faith."

The Lord answered, "If you had faith even as small as a mustard seed, you could say to this mulberry tree, 'May you be uprooted and be planted in the sea,' and it would obey you!"

"When a servant comes in from plowing or taking care of sheep, does his master say, 'Come in and eat with me'? No, he says, 'Prepare my meal, put on your apron, and serve me while I eat. Then you can eat later.' And does the master thank the servant for doing what he was told to do? Of course not. In the same way, when you obey me you should say, 'We are unworthy servants who have simply done our duty.'" — Luke 17:1–10

Jesus said that we are members of a community of servants who are working for a master, and He laid down some rules for His community:

1. Don't do anything to entice other servants to rebel against God; instead, encourage them to obey Him.
2. Resolve conflicts through repentance and forgiveness.
3. Don't think that your service entitles you to God's favor.

The disciples' first response was to demonstrate their lack of faith. They realized that they didn't have what it takes to live up to the standard Jesus set, so God would have to do it if it were to happen. Jesus assured them that they would have power enough to move mountains and continued to describe relationships in the Kingdom of God. His teaching forms the backbone of a transforming relationship, providing us with an outline for the next three sections.

MUTUAL SUBMISSION

The first guideline Jesus gave to His community of servants is that we should never hinder or obstruct others as they pursue a relationship with Him; instead, we should encourage one another to get closer to Him.

Do you remember the passage in Ephesians 5 on being filled with the Holy Spirit? Paul's last admonition in it was for us to submit to one another out of reverence for Christ. In this three-way relationship, both servants submit to Jesus, the Head; then, they submit to one another out of reverence for Him. This command applies in marriage and every other transforming relationship as well. Mutual submission does not take place apart from Jesus Christ.

Going back to the Luke 17 passage, in the example of a master who asks his servant who has come in from the field to serve him dinner, there is a prioritized order of service. The master comes first, then the servants. The Ephesians 5 and Philippians 2 passages add another order of service: serve others first. So it is Jesus first, then others, then self. This pattern achieves mutual submission in transforming relationships. So what is the service that we render to Jesus and others? In Jesus's example, the master is in agriculture, and his servants are working in the field. Our Master has a business, too, and a field. He is in the business of redemption, and His field is the world. The world includes people, institutions, cultures, and nations. We are called to serve as God's agents of redemption in every situation. To the lost, redemption is to bring them to Christ, and for the believer, redemption is to bring them closer to Jesus.

Mutual submission in a transforming relationship demands that I put the redemption of my fellow web-bound servants ahead of my own needs. It doesn't mean that I submit to their wishes, but I should serve their best interest as Jesus determines it. Pure love is taking the time to know someone with such depth that we discover what Jesus wants for them. There has to be communication and agreement between the servants regarding what is best for the other. We don't force our opinion of what is best; instead, we discern it together through the Word of God. For example, I know that lying is never God's will for us, and everyone in the relationship will agree. In a transforming relationship, if my fellow servant is lying, I am sure this is not God's will for him, so I will have to confront him and help him repent. The Bible is clear about most life issues we face; sexual immorality, stealing, murder, and other wickedness is never God's will for us. The first principle of mutual submission in transforming relationships is that Scripture determines God's will for the other person; it is not based on anyone's wishes or opinion. Servants need to study the Bible and get personal guidance from the Holy Spirit to discern God's will for each person within the relationship.[59] It is also critical that we agree that this indeed is God's leading and not just a personal preference.

Mutual submission should not involve trivial matters in life, like what color socks to wear on a given day, though we should seek to avoid any clear violation of Scripture. In many situations, God does give us the freedom to choose what we prefer; it is not always set in stone. In such areas, putting others first translates into acknowledging the freedom God gave them and affirming their choices. When we are close to other servants in a web of transforming relationships, we'll be able to discern the critical issues and learn how to be redemptive agents in their lives.

REBUKE, REPENT, FORGIVE

The second directive Jesus gave is a way to deal with conflict among His servants. It's easy to feel like we're spending too much of our time and energy dealing with conflict in relationships, but conflict can undermine our ministries if not dealt with. This isn't to say conflict should be avoided. If dealt with biblically, conflict can be an asset and strength to any group of people since resolved conflicts are a pathway to unity. The best relationships I am involved in were born out of conflict. Going through the pain of resolving conflict makes a relationship resilient and valuable.

Our teammate, Thomas Liechti, is a peacemaker. God uses him to sense conflict and to resolve it. He has taught a seminar on conflict resolution on several occasions, and I have benefited from this particular ministry God has given him. Following are my notes from a workshop he presented at Access in 2012. I will use his outline and expand it with my thoughts to show how to resolve conflicts:

"If you remember that your brother or sister has something against you..."

---

[59] Romans 12:2.

At the time of this workshop, we observed rising tension over the past year within our team. It hurt our marriage relationships, team relationships, and beyond; we needed to act since this tension was spiritually harmful and contradicted our testimony.

The Word of God commands us to dwell in unity and harmony to have common goals and secure two things: mutual love and mutual grace.

The story of the prodigal son is a blueprint for resolving conflict. Please read it and imagine two believers in the roles of the brothers in this story,

> *To illustrate the point further, Jesus told them this story: "A man had two sons. The younger son told his father, 'I want my share of your estate now before you die.' So his father agreed to divide his wealth between his sons.*
>
> *"A few days later this younger son packed all his belongings and moved to a distant land, and there he wasted all his money in wild living. About the time his money ran out, a great famine swept over the land, and he began to starve. He persuaded a local farmer to hire him, and the man sent him into his fields to feed the pigs. The young man became so hungry that even the pods he was feeding the pigs looked good to him. But no one gave him anything.*
>
> *"When he finally came to his senses, he said to himself, 'At home even the hired servants have food enough to spare, and here I am dying of hunger! I will go home to my father and say, "Father, I have sinned against both heaven and you, and I am no longer worthy of being called your son. Please take me on as a hired servant."'*
>
> *"So he returned home to his father. And while he was still a long way off, his father saw him coming. Filled with love and compassion, he ran to his son, embraced him, and kissed him. His son said to him, 'Father, I have sinned against both heaven and you, and I am no longer worthy of being called your son.'*

"But his father said to the servants, 'Quick! Bring the finest robe in the house and put it on him. Get a ring for his finger and sandals for his feet. And kill the calf we have been fattening. We must celebrate with a feast, for this son of mine was dead and has now returned to life. He was lost, but now he is found.' So the party began.

"Meanwhile, the older son was in the fields working. When he returned home, he heard music and dancing in the house, and he asked one of the servants what was going on. 'Your brother is back,' he was told, 'and your father has killed the fattened calf. We are celebrating because of his safe return.'

"The older brother was angry and wouldn't go in. His father came out and begged him, but he replied, 'All these years I've slaved for you and never once refused to do a single thing you told me to. And in all that time you never gave me even one young goat for a feast with my friends. Yet when this son of yours comes back after squandering your money on prostitutes, you celebrate by killing the fattened calf!'

"His father said to him, 'Look, dear son, you have always stayed by me, and everything I have is yours. We had to celebrate this happy day. For your brother was dead and has come back to life! He was lost, but now he is found!'"

— Luke 15:11–32

We can see the following principles and phases of conflict resolution outlined and illustrated in the story of the prodigal son:

4. REALIZE
    This is a phase of assessment when we become aware of sin. It is an eye-opening experience like the one the prodigal son had when he was feeding the pigs. In this phase, we ask the following questions:

- What is the nature of the problem? Is it an attitude? Words? Behavior or actions?
- What sin is involved? Though we consider problems and criticism as God's tools to bring us to further maturity in Christ, the reality of sin is also involved, which leads to conflict.
- Who is involved? Who is affected? Individual, couple, whole team?

5. RESOLVE

   This is a phase when one or both parties of the conflict decide to end the conflict. In some cases, especially those that involve crime, we should not rush into the decision to end the conflict but proceed carefully and with competent counsel. But in cases where God makes clear that the dispute should end, the goal is reconciliation.

6. REPENT

   Once we decide to resolve the conflict, we must take responsibility for what we did to contribute to the conflict. Taking responsibility is not an exercise in assigning blame but in searching your soul; through the light of the Word of God and the Holy Spirit's help, seek to gain a conviction of the particular sin that helped fuel the conflict. Conflict resolution is most effective when we develop a God-sourced conviction of how we have sinned. Our goal is not to offer a polite response to others nor to be perceived in a certain way but to hear a word from God. Once we receive this conviction that we have sinned, the next step is to repent of it, which means that we agree with God that what we did is wrong and that we will not behave that way again. Conviction, regret, and determination are involved in repentance.

   Be careful in this soul search not to allow false guilt and self-abasement to become driving forces in your repentance. Satan is the accuser, and he will take every opportunity to discourage you and make you give up serving the Lord. One way I can tell the difference between conviction from the Holy Spirit and discouraging thoughts is that the Spirit's message usually comes from a passage of Scripture. Also, God never insults me. He reveals His truth tenderly, precisely, and accurately. He doesn't condemn me with general accusations. God's conviction sounds like this: "When you said such and such, you were not telling the truth. You need to correct that. Call the person and tell them the truth."

7. RETURN

After we have prayed and repented of the sin of which God convicted us, it is time to take the initiative and reapproach the other person. A trusted third person could help set up the meeting. In the meeting, tell the person, "God convicted me that when I did such and such, I was wrong. It was a sin, and I have repented of it before God, and now I am here to ask for your forgiveness." Do this without giving reasons or describing the circumstances that led to your sin. Now, move on to what the other person has done or said to hurt you. Do this without accusations or general statements of judgment and condemnation. Say something like, "When you said such and such, it hurt my feelings." If the Bible calls what the other person did a sin, use the passage to confront them with it. For example, "Leviticus 19:11 says, 'do not lie.' You told me that you wrote the report when, in fact, someone else did."

On the other hand, if the Bible does not clearly define the offense, say, "The tone of the words hurt my feelings." Notice that neither the word "you" nor its derivatives belong in this sentence. Then allow them to respond.

If someone else initiated the conflict resolution and approached you, be open to criticism. An excellent way to accept any critical comment is to think of it as free personal or professional advice.5

8. RECONCILE

If both sides are ready to express repentance and forgiveness, verbalize it to each other. It may be helpful to verbalize the offense first and then pronounce forgiveness to each other. Pronounce forgiveness in the name of Jesus Christ to the other explicitly and in detail.

9. RECLOTHE

After forgiveness, in this phase, speak of the other person's value and the relationship that connects you. Affirm them with words that show their worth, how God has made them unique. Give verbal affirmation that you are not holding any offense for a future accusation.

10. REJOICE

Celebrate together and involve the team in a feast!

ENTITLEMENT AND EXPECTATIONS

The third directive Jesus gave to His community of servants deals with an issue of the heart. He said, "When you obey me, you should say, 'We are unworthy servants who have simply done our duty'" (Luke 17:10). God does not owe us anything in exchange for our obedience. But when we obey Jesus and make sacrifices for the sake of others, we are prone to develop an attitude of entitlement.

In 1999, I was on my way from Qarnayel to Aley, and in the car with me was Sandy, our kids, and a friend visiting from the US. A car passed me and stopped right in front of our car, blocking our way. I had to stop. A man with bloodshot eyes leaped out of the car with a club in his hand. He ran toward me and tried to reach through my window to hit me in the face. I blocked him with my left arm. He used the stick to strike me six times on my left arm before a crowd gathered around and pulled him away from my car. I did nothing to provoke the attack. The Syrian army was in control in Lebanon, and there was no rule of law. Local militias had a free run, and if you knew the right people, you could get away with anything. Someone at the scene of the incident called the army, and they came and arrested both of us. They took me from one army barrack to another, then to prison in Beirut, where I spent the night. They placed me in a 20 by 20–foot room. There were 72 other men crammed in there—I had time to count them several times. Everyone was standing since there was nothing to sit on and no room to lie down. Not that you'd want to lie down, because the restroom overflow covered the floor with a half-inch layer of what I presume was sewage. I met a young man accused of rape, and he described what had happened in general terms. He knew he was guilty. We talked for a couple of hours, I shared the gospel with him, and then he laid down on the floor, used an empty Coke bottle as a pillow, and went to sleep. It was about midnight, and soon everyone had to lie down, so it was a pile of men lying in sewage until morning. I chose a spot farthest from the restroom with my back against a wall and settled down for the night. I had a long conversation with the Lord that I still remember today. I was angry at the man who attacked me, at the Syrian army, at the Lebanese army who arrested me, and at all the people of the Middle East. I no longer wanted to preach the good news to them; they deserved hell, and I was ready to let them have it. But I was most angry with God. How could He let this happen to me? Didn't He promise that if I followed Him, He would be my protector? What kind of Father would do this to His son? I was angry with God, and I let Him know it. As I poured out my heart to God, I began to connect the dots from my experience to what He allowed others to do to Jesus, and I realized that my suffering was nothing compared to His. The Lord asked me, *Will you love the people of Lebanon?*

I replied with all sincerity, "No, I hate the Lebanese and the Syrians, and all people as well."

Then the Lord spoke to me again and said, *would you do it for Me?*

I replied, "For you, Lord, I'll do anything. Yes, I will love them."

The night I spent in prison helped me rediscover my Master. I gained a new awareness that I serve Him first and others because of Him. This experience also convicted me of having a bad attitude of entitlement. I thought I was entitled to a safe life, free of significant tragedy and suffering. Surely, as God's servant, I'd receive preferential treatment. I expected Him to answer my prayers more often than most because I was laying my life on the line for Him. Do you hear the pride in this attitude? So, I confessed my sin and repented of it; nothing in my life is off-limits to God, and my service to Him does not entitle me to comfort or safety.

I was naïve about people; I didn't know that we are so evil and unlovable. Any plans or efforts built on hope in them or our love for each other are wood, hay, and stubble, and they will not last. What did I expect when I went to Lebanon? Did I think people would roll out the red carpet and shower me with rose petals? I don't expect that anymore, and I take Jesus's words more seriously that if they hate me, they hated Him first (John 15:18). But what about believers? Shouldn't they be different? Yes, if they are submitted servants of the Master; otherwise, they'll act just like people of the world.

I was released the next day around 11 a.m. with an apology. It seems it took them that long to figure out that I had done nothing wrong. Later, a close friend told me that he heard that a local militia boss had ordered the man with the club to attack me. A year earlier, Sandy and I had started Access Technical School in Aley, as well as a new church of Druze believers called The Lord's Family. My friend was sure that the attacker intended to intimidate us and get us to leave the area.

In a transforming relationship, servants need to maintain a thankful attitude toward God without expecting perfection from each other or righteousness from the world; otherwise, disappointment will continuously haunt them. Even the best people who look fantastic on the outside have extremely troubling insides. By engaging in intimate relationships with broken people, we get to see their hearts and love them no matter what we find. Of course, the reverse is also true. Those in close association with us have to love us despite the disgusting mess they see. We adopt the attitude that Jesus wants us to have through a miracle that God performs in us, and it is transformational.

CHAPTER EIGHT
TRANSFORMATION IN WORSHIP

Here is a fantastic principle: God created humans to become like the one they worship; you are who you worship! What you set your heart on, what you meditate on—that is the likeness into which you will be transformed. This principle is the reason behind the first of the Ten Commandments, "You must not have any other god but me" (Exodus 20:3). Whatever occupies our hearts and engages our fancy is what we worship. Idol worship is prevalent everywhere in the world. It manifests in religion and other firmly held beliefs, holding the human spirit in bondage and keeping it from entering the presence of God. Any action not performed as worship to God is idolatry; even Christian ministry amounts to idolatry when it is not initiated by God nor carried out as a service to Him.

God created us for worship, and we cannot help but do so. The question is, will we bow down to God or the whims and desires of our own heart? In a moment of decision, the first choice we have to make is to worship God. Worship and transformation go hand in hand; they are the fruit of the same transaction between God and the believer.

When Jesus and the disciples were traveling on foot from Judea to Galilee, they passed through the region of the Samaritans, who were part-Jews despised by the rest of Israel. They stopped at Jacob's well near a village called Sychar, and here Jesus had a fascinating conversation with a woman:[60]

> *When a Samaritan woman came to draw water, Jesus said to her, "Will you give me a drink?" (His disciples had gone into the town to buy food.)*
>
> *The Samaritan woman said to him, "You are a Jew and I am a Samaritan woman. How can you ask me for a drink?" (For Jews do not associate with Samaritans.)*
>
> *Jesus answered her, "If you knew the gift of God and who it is that asks you for a drink, you would have asked him and he would have given you living water."*
>
> *"Sir," the woman said, "you have nothing to draw with and the well is deep. Where can you get this living water? Are you greater than our father Jacob, who gave us the well and drank from it himself, as did also his sons and his livestock?"*
>
> *Jesus answered, "Everyone who drinks this water will be thirsty again, but whoever drinks the water I give them will never thirst. Indeed, the water I give them will become in them a spring of water welling up to eternal life."*
>
> *The woman said to him, "Sir, give me this water so that I won't get thirsty and have to keep coming here to draw water."*
>
> *He told her, "Go, call your husband and come back."*
>
> *"I have no husband," she replied.*

---

[60] Jesus broke several traditions by going through Samaria and speaking to a Samaritan woman. For a summary of the historical background to this story, see www.biblestudytools.com/bible-study/topical-studies/the-samaritans-hope-from-the-history-of-a-hated-people.html.

Jesus said to her, "You are right when you say you have no husband. The fact is, you have had five husbands, and the man you now have is not your husband. What you have just said is quite true."

"Sir," the woman said, "I can see that you are a prophet. Our ancestors worshiped on this mountain, but you Jews claim that the place where we must worship is in Jerusalem."

"Woman," Jesus replied, "believe me, a time is coming when you will worship the Father neither on this mountain nor in Jerusalem. You Samaritans worship what you do not know; we worship what we do know, for salvation is from the Jews. Yet a time is coming and has now come when the true worshipers will worship the Father in the Spirit and in truth, for they are the kind of worshipers the Father seeks. God is spirit, and his worshipers must worship in the Spirit and in truth."

The woman said, "I know that Messiah" (called Christ) "is coming. When he comes, he will explain everything to us."

Then Jesus declared, "I, the one speaking to you—I am he."

— John 4:7–26 NIV

There is so much happening in this conversation, but I want to focus on the discussion of worship. The woman wanted Jesus to settle an argument between Jews and Samaritans regarding the proper place of worship. Samaritans worshiped on Mt. Gerizim, while the Jews worshiped on the Temple Mount, or Mt. Moriah, in Jerusalem. Who was more aligned with God's will? Jesus responded that neither location was truly important anymore. He explained to the woman that God the Father is Spirit and that He is seeking true worshippers, who worship Him in spirit and truth. No matter where our bodies are located, we offer true worship to God in our spirit and with the Word of God. The reason we worship in spirit is that God is Spirit! It is a communication from the human spirit to God's Spirit, and outward actions reflect this spiritual connection.

THE PRESENCE OF GOD

The Old Testament books of Exodus, Leviticus, Deuteronomy, and Numbers provide instructions to Jacob's descendants on how to worship God. God spoke to Moses in great detail about making the tabernacle and the Ark of the Covenant, and He gave supernatural skill to specific artisans in Israel for that very purpose. He also spelled out to them how and when to offer sacrifices, and He specified the people who were allowed to do it. All that labor and detail was necessary for one person to enter the presence of God on behalf of a whole nation. Through Jesus Christ and His sacrifice on the cross, all the laws and ordinances given to Moses are satisfied, and we can now enter the presence of God individually and communally at any moment— what a profound mystery is the cross of Jesus Christ!

There is a holy place in the believer, a spiritual room, where we meet with God in the presence of His Holy Spirit through the Word of God. It is the same place where we make choices in a moment of decision. When we enter into this holy place, we enter into the presence of God; here, our spirit beholds Him, hears His voice, and He hears us. This is how the apostle Paul describes coming into the presence of God:

> *But whenever someone turns to the Lord, the veil is taken away. For the Lord is the Spirit, and wherever the Spirit of the Lord is, there is freedom. So all of us who have had that veil removed can see and reflect the glory of the Lord. And the Lord—who is the Spirit—makes us more and more like him as we are changed into his glorious image.*
>
> *— 2 Corinthians 3:16–18*

The essence of worship is to see and reflect the glory of God.[61] In our spirit, we can enter the presence of God, see Him, and reflect His glory back to Him and onward to others. The apostle adds that as we look at the glory of God, He transforms us into His image! The presence of God is where and how transformation takes place.

In our church, The Lord's Family, we faced the question of defining a disciple of Jesus Christ. The Great Commission is to make disciples of all nations, not merely convert, so we needed to determine our goal's parameters. It was also confusing to know who was a true disciple of Jesus Christ because many professed Christ as a way to get help from the church. Christian literature offers us some discipleship indicators, including daily devotional practices and testifying to God's love. The problem with such standards is that we knew many who spent regular time in the Word of God, recited eloquent public prayers, and even witnessed to others about Jesus Christ, yet they did not reflect the likeness of God in their lives.

I came across a similar situation during my years of training with the Navigators, known for their excellent discipleship programs. Yet, some believers could go through the prescribed disciplines without ever entering the presence of God. Others struggled to make progress; discipleship seemed a task and a competition reserved for spiritual giants. I saw many silently withdraw from the team because they felt defeated. The disciplines themselves are lovely, giving power to the believer, but they don't turn one into a disciple. A believer becomes a disciple by spending time in the presence of God. This is the simple definition we use in The Lord's Family for a disciple: someone who comes into God's presence regularly.

At our school in Aley, the presence of Jesus Christ is an integral part of our teaching philosophy and practice. The teacher is a disciple who leads students into the presence of God in the classroom. In this approach, transformative education takes place in the holy place in the heart of believers. Teaching becomes an act of worship for the community of administrators, teachers, students, and, whenever possible, the parents.

_____

[61] In Let the Nations Be Glad, John Piper says that the essence of worship is the experience of being satisfied with God in Christ. I prefer the definition that worship is to see and reflect God's glory because it keeps God at the center, not human satisfaction. The greatest act of worship ever performed was the death of Jesus Christ on the cross. It was a selfless act of obedience to the Father, even if it meant being abandoned.

The history books of the Old Testament show us a pattern that whenever people entered the presence of God, they were changed, and then God used them in mighty ways. Abraham, Moses, Gideon, David, Daniel, and others—entered the presence of God by faith and were transformed into the people God intended them to be.

THE ACT OF WORSHIP

The book *How to Worship Jesus Christ* by Joseph S. Carroll introduced me to the idea that worship can consist of actions and prayers lifted to God. A significant contribution it has made in my life is to move my perception of worship from the outward—the actions of devotion—to the inward realm of the spirit. Our actions are rooted in our heart attitudes. Here again, we see the connection between thoughts and actions. The actions that spring from true worship to God are the works He had planned for us; these bear much fruit, and they endure forever. All other works, no matter how good they seem on the outside, will fade away.

Sandy and I have three sons and a daughter. When they were children, they wanted to buy us presents on our birthdays, so I'd give them the money they needed. They wanted to express their love for us but had no means of their own to do it. Since we had to pay for the gifts, were they gifts at all? Not in a financial sense, but the love behind the gesture was deeply meaningful to us. In a similar fashion to my children's request, I have often asked my heavenly Father, "What can I give you, Lord, as an expression of my love?" That question leads me to ponder why God asks us to do anything for Him when He can do it better Himself. After all, anything we do apart from Him is worthless, so anything good we do is, in reality, Him doing it through us. Is there anything that I can give to God that is uniquely from me, something that He wouldn't have otherwise? It is my love expressed in worship. God is not dependent on me or anything I do, so my devotion to Him is the only value I can add to life. Teaching, evangelizing, praying, serving, and all other acts of ministry are the product of a partnership between God and me; I offer the worship, and He provides everything I need to do the works for which He has called me.

In 1997, Sandy and I were driving from Qarnayel to Aley on the upper road, through Hammana and Sawfar. It was April, and on our way up the shoulder of Kaniset Mountain, overlooking the La Martine valley, we saw a tide of clouds coming in from the Mediterranean. It was a sight to behold; standing above the clouds, they looked like giant cotton balls filling the valley. The scene was so majestic and overwhelming that we had to stop the car, get out, and worship God. We stood by the side of the road, gazed out at the whole valley of clouds sprawled out beneath us, sang several songs, and remembered the confession, "The chief end of man is to glorify God and enjoy Him forever." We then began to praise God in prayer. As if in response, the clouds opened up to reveal a flock of sheep grazing right beneath us, and then another flock came up the slope from the valley and joined them. At that sight, the Lord spoke to my spirit, saying, *You worship; I will gather.* This word from God is why worship is the first core value of our ministry at Access. Faith in Jesus Christ and transformation into His likeness are miraculous works of God, not something we do in our strength. All we contribute in our ministry is worship to God, which takes the form of praise, prayers, teaching and Bible study, service to others, acts of kindness, counseling, encouragement, and mutual submission. Establishing new churches begins and persists with worship. The centrality of worship is emphasized throughout the Word of God; witness the procession of praise that brought down Jericho's walls,[62] and see how God assured the defeat of King David's enemies. Those who worship God accomplish the work of God.

Service to God as an act of worship is transformative. It puts us in the appropriate role in our relationship with God and changes our attitudes and relationships with others. Service as worship leaves no room for pride or selfish ambition, and it results in works that glorify God alone.

---

[62] Joshua 6:1–27.

CHAPTER NINE
TRANSFORMATION THROUGH OUR CALLING

The promise to Abraham and his household is that God will bless them *and* make them a blessing to all nations. The second part of the promise, to be a blessing to the nations, is key. In heaven we will be able to do everything we do here, only better, with one notable exception: only here on earth can we share the gospel with others. The lost will not be in heaven, so if we want to save them, now is the time to do it.

For the Blessing to spread to all nations, the Kingdom of God must come to reign in the life of every individual, community, and human institution in existence. And it must spread even further to include all creation, which is burdened by sin and awaiting liberty at the revelation of Jesus Christ. Sharing the Blessing of the Kingdom of God brings healing to the environment and restores a world that was corrupted by sin.

God gave us a role in the Kingdom's irruption into the world, and we refer to it as our calling. There is a general calling that applies to all believers, and there a specific calling for individuals and teams. Together, our general and specific callings define what our actions ought to be during our time in this world, and they serve as one of the powerful forces that transform us into the likeness of Jesus Christ.

OUR GENERAL CALLING

In Ephesians 1 and 2, the apostle Paul states that God's purpose is to bring everything into subjection to Jesus Christ in the Church. The Church is the vehicle that the Father wishes to use to subject all things to the Son. In Chapter 3, the apostle gives us his response to this revelation of the "mystery" of the Church. He describes his ministry in two parts:

- "To preach to the gentiles" (3:8)
- "To bring to light what is the administration of the mystery" (3:9)

The first element of Paul's ministry is a capsule of the Great Commission since preaching involves going, evangelizing others, and teaching them to observe Jesus' commands. The second element is a reference to church planting. The "mystery" is the Church, in which Jews and Gentiles join Christ in one body. "Bringing to light the administration of that mystery" refers to how God, through the leaders He ordains, sets up the physical manifestation of the body in a specific location. The word "administration" refers to the enactment in time and space of the mystery.

This passage is central to our philosophy of ministry since it shows a clear link between the Great Commission and church planting. The Great Commission is Jesus's plan of action for accomplishing the Father's purpose. Before we look at the content of the plan, here are some key observations:

- God gave the plan to the Church through the apostles. So it is a plan for the whole Church, not just a select group of individuals. The Church is the vessel in which all things, including people, are being brought into subjection to Jesus Christ.
- The plan is for every people group on Earth. There are already many churches among many people groups. However, many groups still have no churches, especially the Muslims and Jews of North Africa and the Middle East.
- The plan is a reproductive process. The act of "teaching them to observe all that Jesus has commanded" implies that discipleship is

incomplete until we pass on the command and function of making disciples of all nations (2 Timothy 2:22).

- The plan gives the Church the responsibility of "teaching to observe all that Jesus has commanded."

It is essential to distinguish between "teaching to observe" and teaching in general. Teaching is the effective communication of information and ideas. However, teaching to observe involves the submission of the will to result in a new behavior. In other words, transformation (Romans 12:2) is a required part of the plan.

- The plan, when implemented, is, in effect, a Great Commission to plant churches. Only the Church can make disciples; in fact, this action defines the life and mission of the Church. Also, according to the plan, the newly planted church is one that produces reproducing churches.
- The plan is a commission by the authority of Jesus, who has all authority in heaven and earth. Jesus' presence and power are available to the Church for executing the plan. It is the plan of His choice for a limited time, namely until the "end of the age."

The content of the plan is to make disciples of all ethnic groups through three imperatives:

1. Going
2. Evangelizing
3. Teaching to observe

The first imperative of the plan refers to the Church being in the world but not of it. It beckons the Church to find its place in the world, managing to be distinct but not isolating itself from unbelievers. As the Church relates to the world, it has to take the initiative to cross physical, cultural, and spiritual barriers and establish a credible presence with every people group. This seemingly simple one-word function has had many difficulties associated with it. Before a disciple can get "going," he or she must receive education about the destination, learn the language, learn to translate God's Word and raise financial support. Then, once among the new people group, the disciple must navigate cross-cultural living and communication while recruiting helpers from the community. So merely going isn't enough. *How* the church goes to all nations has a direct impact on the second element of the plan.

"Baptizing them in the name of the Father, and the Son, and the Holy Spirit" is the crowning moment of evangelism. Once we have proclaimed the gospel to the nations and added those who believe to the Church, we mark the joyous event with water baptism. This imperative raises an essential point regarding underground churches and believers who keep their faith secret. Baptism is a public proclamation made by the believer, signifying that they have left the kingdom of darkness and joined God's Kingdom.

The third imperative is to teach those who have been baptized to observe all that Jesus commanded us. It involves teaching and preaching, fellowship, accountability, equipping, modeling, and mentoring. It also includes training and sending missionaries to continue the reproductive cycle of church planting.

The plan describes both the life and the mission of the Church. By fulfilling these roles, the Church lives out its identity and achieves its goal of making disciples of all nations. Church planting among the nations proceeds with a clear understanding of Jesus's plan. It is not just a way of doing things or an idea for reaching the nations. It is nothing less than His plan. It is the basis of the Church's missionary strategy, to the exclusion of personal visions and agendas of individuals within the church.

The plan directly impacts the dynamic of relationships within a missionary team. The team's goal is not a mandate passed down by the leader or an organization, but what the Lord has commanded and authorized the Church to do. Once a church makes known its mission to its members and the members understand the plan, the Lord calls out some for service on a church-planting team. The next step for those with such a calling is for them to prepare for service.

The Great Commission is a general calling for every believer in Jesus Christ, and it confers on us a common template for life in the world:

- We have one Head, Jesus Christ, and we are His servants, sent by Him and endued with His authority.
- We are not alone, but members of a household, and our calling is only part of the overall task assigned to us by Jesus Christ.
- The writer of Hebrews says of the people of faith who preceded us, "All these people earned a good reputation because of their faith, yet none of them received all that God had promised. For God had something better in mind for us, so that they would not reach perfection without us" (Hebrews 11:39–40). Our lives are planted in the context of the history of the household of God. He does not call us to isolated tasks but to a labor of love that began a long time ago. What we do and say builds on and adds to that story. Our story and work are not complete until everyone has contributed their part, and then, together, we fulfill our destiny.
- The call to the nations imposes an outward focus for the Church and us individually. We are in this world primarily for others, not ourselves. When we incorporate this element into our life goals and plans, transformation is a certainty.

OUR SPECIFIC CALLING

Sandy and I are part of a small group that meets on Thursday nights. Two couples in the group, Jim and Peggy Eby and Ken and Sharon Womack, founded Mission Catalyst International. The website describes their mission as "primarily equipping and mobilizing indigenous missionaries and church planters in the Majority World to more effectively evangelize, disciple, and plant churches among the least-reached peoples of the earth. Our passion is to help see *The Great Commission* completed in this generation."

In one of our meetings, Jim and Peggy shared a message they heard at church from Ephesians. In the passage, the apostle Paul affirms, "For we are God's handiwork, created in Christ Jesus to do good works, which God prepared in advance for us to do" (Ephesians 2:10 NIV). Jim explained that the Greek word translated "handiwork" is *poiēma*, the root from which the word "poem" is derived. I was impressed with the idea Paul was communicating in that verse: we are each a unique creation of God, and

He has prepared a unique set of works for each one of us to do. It is not a cookie-cutter production bench but the strokes of an artist that shape us into who we are. Our transformation is unique, and the works He calls us to are as well.

In writing this book, my goal is to inspire you to find that one-of-a-kind transformed poiēma that God authored you to be. It is not a call to generic change in which one size fits all, and this makes it imperative that we each determine our specific calling and set of works that God has prepared for us. It is also critical to realize that God embeds our particular calling in a broader and more encompassing team calling.

From 2008 to 2011, I served as co–area director of missionary teams for North Africa and the Middle East in a large mission agency. One of my responsibilities was to oversee and train team leaders. We decided on a two-phase training approach. First, we gathered team leader couples and asked them to tell their story. Each person had several hours to go into as much detail as they felt led to, and the rest of us listened. We took notes and repeated what we heard, allowing the storyteller to clarify and retell their story. We then prayed for them and asked God to give us a verse from the Bible that fit their life story. We spent the whole week doing nothing but this. Invariably, the storyteller cried while they told their story, and each one came away with a verse that described what God was saying through them.

In the next phase, we asked the team leaders to tell the story that God spoke through them as a community. God weaves together our individual stories and reveals His glory in a way that no individual can do alone.

I always repeated this exercise in our leadership training. I found that it gave people a clear vision of their purpose, transforming them into single-minded and focused leaders for Jesus Christ. The exercise helped people discern the goal of their relationship with God, both as individuals and as a group. It also bonded them together in one story, united by God's purpose for them as a group.

The Access Team went through a similar process of identifying the team members' specific callings and then discerning a calling for the group as a whole. My specific calling is to shepherd the household of God. As a shepherd, I help provide food and water and protect the flock from threats. In church ministry, this translates into giving vision and direction for the church, leading them into the presence of God, teaching the Word of God, and confronting sin when it sneaks in. Another team member has a specific calling to be a peacemaker and another to provide loyalty, which is like a glue that holds the team together. Together we work in harmony to build up the church.

We have discerned that God has called the Access Team to provide the means for all North Africa and the Middle East cultures to express the gospel of Jesus Christ in their own culture and pass it on to others through transforming relationships.

When we determine the specific callings of individuals and teams, the tangible outcomes are unity, strength through diversity, and the ability to discern God's direction. I will elaborate more on each of these in my next book, *Transforming Community*, but I mention them here because I want to point out the power of transformation that each contains.

A NEW PATH

After I graduated from Syracuse University in 1983, I enrolled in a Ph.D. program at Rice University Biology Department. I was interested in neuroscience, so I joined a lab and started researching, mapping neuronal pathways of visual signals in crustaceans. Two years later, I published an article in the Journal of Comparative Physiology, showing the organized structure of photoreceptors and their correlation to their function in channeling e-vector information in the crayfish eye. I enjoyed neuroscience research, but I wanted to accomplish other more important things in my lifetime.

While at Rice University, I joined the Houston Navigators ministry. I was part of a team whose purpose was to establish a Navigator ministry on the University of Houston campus. I started an evangelistic Bible study in one of the dorms, and eleven players on the Cougars football team attended. My relationship with Jesus caused such a transformation in my life that I felt I had to tell others. I had a message not only for individuals but for the nations as well. What happened next made it clear that God had a plan for my life other than neuroscience.

In 1985, a group of fourteen other men from various Texas cities and I traveled to China for a five-week biking trip in south China. Roy

Robertson, a veteran missionary, and the Houston Navigators leader, Kay Crumby, organized the trip. We were supposed to meet in Los Angeles at LAX and fly together to Hong Kong. Unfortunately for the three of us flying out of Houston, our plane's jet engine caught on fire just as we were taking off. The pilot aborted takeoff and returned to the terminal safely, where we waited for seven hours for another flight to take us to LAX. We missed the connection with the other 12 men and flew directly to Hong Kong. When we arrived at the Hong Kong airport, we had no idea where to go and no phone numbers or hotel names to find the others. We walked out of the airport and hopped on a train to a crowded street. We wandered the streets and prayed to God for a way to find the others. As we walked, we came across a church building, so we went in and found the pastor's office. It turned out he not only knew Roy Robertson, but he had heard that Roy was coming with a group of men for this summer trip. He made a couple of phone calls and connected us with the group. He also gave us Chinese names to help people remember us; mine was "Lobesin" because it sounded like Robby. Finding the group in Hong Kong was like finding a needle in a haystack; we knew in our hearts that this was no coincidence but that the hand of God was with us.

We purchased bicycles in Hong Kong and took a ferry to Guangzhou, and then we boarded a train for a marathon nineteen-hour train ride to Guilin. From there, we started bicycling back toward Guangzhou, stopping in different cities, and preaching the good news of the gospel to those who would listen. None of us spoke any Chinese. Roy knew a few words, just enough to share the Navigator's Bridge Illustration in Cantonese. Mike, who could draw well, taught us how to quickly draw ducks and pigs on napkins when ordering food at restaurants. We were riding between ninety and a hundred kilometers per day. In one of the cities along the way, I decided to go for a bike ride alone to discover the area. I came to a scenic bridge and stood there for a while. A crowd started gathering around me for no apparent reason, but I think it was because they knew I was a foreigner. A woman came close, so I took out a gospel tract and asked her to read it aloud. I repeated every phrase she spoke, and the crowd of about thirty people cheered me on as I tried to speak their language. At the end of the gospel presentation, I shouted several times, "Nee dow gaw?" which meant, do you want to pray? The woman who read the pamphlet prayed along with several others. One person on the periphery of the gathering looked at me angrily and yelled at me. The group hushed her and told her to run along.

A couple of weeks into the journey, we wandered into a Ping Lo village and checked into the only hotel. Several locals came up to me to feel the hair on my arms and chest because they hadn't seen people like us before. The second day at Ping Lo, a woman who spoke English came from what seemed to be a faraway city to communicate what the officials wanted to say to us. They said we had entered a forbidden area of China where foreigners were not allowed. They also said they would load our bikes in a dump truck and put us on a bus to take us out of the region. They searched our backpacks, which were full of Chinese gospel tracts and Bibles, and confiscated it all—except for the items in my bag. Although they searched my bag too, they didn't seize any of the literature I had; they let me keep all of it. The group leaders, Roy and Kay, were 62 and 53 years old, respectively, so it would make sense for the party officials to address them, but they didn't look at them; they looked at me, and they warned me, "Do not preach the gospel to anyone. You are not allowed." Roy interrupted them and said to the translator that Chinese law allowed sharing the gospel. I don't think she translated his comments to them. The officials directed their conversation to me, which was surprising since I was neither the oldest nor the group leader.

They shipped us out through the southern border of the region, released us, and returned our bikes, and we continued our journey south toward Guangzhou. We spent the final two weeks in Guangzhou, where I met different people in the parks, restaurants, and streets. Many of the people in this city spoke English, so I communicated more clearly with them. Two here, three there, I prayed with 17 in all to receive Jesus Christ. On our last day in Guangzhou, eleven of them, who didn't know each other, came to see me at the hotel. I introduced them to one another and spent three hours going over the gospel with them and sharing the Wheel Illustration from the Navigators. The next day we left mainland China and went to Macao for two days and then returned home to Houston.

In the following two years, I received several letters from the new believers in Guangzhou. Seven of them continued to meet together, and they started a new church that grew beyond my wildest imagination. God had my attention. The lesson I learned is that His power flowed through my life when I was going about His business.

My supervising professor at Rice University was not happy that I took several weeks off to go to China. He said I had to put neuroscience first in my life, or he would not support me in my quest for a doctorate. I had come to know my professor well, and although he was a brilliant man, I did not want to model my life after his, so I left the Ph.D. program, settled for a master's degree in Neuroscience, and began preparing for a career in missions.

The experience of God's power flowing through me during the China trip, weak as I was, was a milestone in my transformation journey. I was able to go into God's presence, and there He showed me His heart for the world and His plan for my life. He made me a member of His family and was in the process of revealing His calling on my life.

A NEW FAMILY

Leaving Satan and cleaving to the Father of Jesus Christ means becoming a member of the household of God, the community of God. We become partakers of the divine nature, as the apostle Peter tells us in 1 Peter 1. He's not saying that we become God, but that through His promises, He has made way for us to join Him in the community of God.

Membership in this community means our relationships are formed and lived out based on how the Father, Son, and Holy Spirit relate to each other and us. The way they relate to each other determines how we interact in the household. John 17, which is often called the High Priestly Prayer of Jesus, sheds light on the web of relationships in the household of God.

Transformation through creation cannot happen outside the household of God, and no set of principles or practices can circumvent this requirement. Neither Bible Study nor prayer and fasting nor any other spiritual discipline will be able to transform us apart from relationships in the body of Christ. As it was in the lives of Abraham, Isaac, and Jacob, God uses the relationships within His house to transform everyone in it. Here is an important principle to underscore: God uses relationships to transform us.

God has a specific place and role for each member of His house. It is not random nor generic, but specific to each one. He customizes our lives to transform us into unique messengers of His glory that fit together to form a complete love story. The position and role we have are part of the story of God's family, put into action by the promises made to Abraham. They determine our purpose in life and guide us into discerning the good works He has prepared for us.[63] We can think of transformation as the process by which we find our part of the story and learn to tell it.

After I came back from China, planting churches became my passion. In my transformation story, the Lord led me to meet Sandy in 1985. Kay Crumby planned a dinner at a Chinese restaurant in downtown Houston to share about the summer trip with the donors who made it possible. I was one of several who spoke at the dinner. After my presentation, a young lady named Sandy came by and asked me more questions about the trip and what it was like to share the gospel in China. She was in one of the Navigators Bible study groups in the Houston area, but I had never met her before. Sandy found out about the dinner from a newsletter her mother received from Kay Crumby. When her mother saw my picture in Kay's newsletter, she exclaimed, "What's a Lebanese Navigator from Texas doing in China?"

A week after the China presentation dinner, I saw Sandy again at our singles' Sunday school class at Spring Branch Community Church. She was visiting our church by invitation from her Bible study leader and happened to be at the singles class. We talked about missions and discipleship, and she told me that God was calling her to go to the nations. At the time, I lived in a house with three other men in the Navigators ministry in Houston; we were all in our mid-twenties and training to make disciples of all nations. Those were great days that formed a strong foundation for my walk with Jesus Christ, and I am forever grateful to Kay and all the other Navigators who led so many and inspired us to love others and obey God.

One night as I lay in bed, I asked God to send me to the nations. I had enjoyed a taste of what He could do when I was in China, and I wanted Him to do it again. I prayed for my new Chinese brothers and sisters whom I had met over the previous summer and kept in touch in

---

[63] Ephesians 2:10.

letters. As I prayed, I sensed the presence of the Lord, and He affirmed me in my desire to go to the nations to start new churches. I had so many questions about how it would all happen, like how I would make a living, but a profound sense of peace settled my heart. I had confidence that He would bring things together.

Along with the peace, God gave me another thought; He said it was not suitable for me to go alone but that I would need a partner, a wife. Right away, I thought of Sandy. In addition to being drop-dead beautiful, gentle, and kind, she was going in the same direction I was, and God was speaking to her in the same way He was talking to me. What else could I want in a woman? I prayed for a clear direction from God and then went to sleep. The next day, one of my roommates, Mike, said he wanted to ask Lori, Sandy's Bible study leader, to go on a date with him; he wondered if I wanted to ask someone out and make it a double date. He had never asked me that question before, but I said sure. I asked Lori for Sandy's phone number, called Sandy, and she said yes.

The four of us went out to dinner at Paisano's Italian Restaurant on Hillcroft and SW Freeway. While at dinner, we set a time for the four of us to go horseback riding, only for Mike to drop out two days before. When I called Sandy and told her, she said she'd still like to go even if the others couldn't be there. I had been in the horseback riding club at Syracuse University, so I looked forward to getting back in the saddle. But the trail horses they used were not like the trained jumping horses I had ridden before. These horses had a mind of their own and just wanted to go around the trail and head back for home. On our way around the trail, we talked about God's calling and felt complete harmony.

As we headed back to the stalls, I realized we had been walking the horses the whole way, and we hadn't cantered or run. So I decided to fix that. I turned my horse around, away from the stalls, and sent him running. About seven seconds later, my horse realized he was running away from the stalls, and that wasn't part of his program, so he suddenly dug his forehooves in the ground and came to a halt. Naturally, I kept traveling in a trajectory over his head and onto the ground. I am proud to say that I never let go of the reins. I got up, wiped the dust off my clothes, and got back on the horse; in the distance, I could see Sandy trying really hard not to laugh. I learned a valuable lesson from the horse that a hope deferred makes the soul sick. The end of the trail had been in the horse's sight, and I snatched the hope out from his hooves.

After the second date, I took a month to pray to make sure that Sandy was the right person for me. I then phoned her and asked her out again. She was surprised because she hadn't heard from me for a month. On our next date, she asked me, "Why are you dating me?"

I answered her, "To see if you are the right person for me to marry." It was a perfectly reasonable response within my Lebanese culture, but these words were shocking to her. We prayed and asked God for direction, and we sensed Him leading us closer to Him and each other. A few weeks after we met, we became engaged; then, we married on May 16, 1987.

Moments of decision over many years result in a transformed life. The time I spent in God's presence and the calling which I received from Him by faith have shaped my life and destiny. Our choices of career, who we marry, and who we befriend contribute to what we become.

A career in missions does not make a calling more spiritual, or Kingdom centered than any other calling. God has many plans for many people, and they are all different. What does make a calling truly spiritual is when the person called maintains an attitude of worship.

Our calling in life and ministry is like railroad tracks on which the train of our life travels. If we make our choices putting God first, He will transform us into what He intended us to be.

CHAPTER TEN

TRANSFORMATION THROUGH INNER HEALING AND DELIVERANCE

In 1989, Sandy and I decided to attend a weekend conference on marriage in Austin, Texas. The conference was led and taught by Dr. and Mrs. Ferguson, who would later write a book based on these teachings called Intimate Encounters. We have significantly benefited from their training and have passed it on to others in our marriage seminars at Access. I remember at the first meeting of the conference, Dr. Ferguson drew a circle on the board and said, "This represents your soul, which is your mind, will, and emotions. If you have lost a significant person in your life—a parent, spouse, or child—draw a line down the middle of the circle. Now, this is you." I looked at the half-circle, wrestling with this idea that my soul was incomplete. But I had to admit it was true: when I lost my father, I lost half of me. When I came to Christ and embraced my heavenly Father, He made me whole again, but my soul still needed healing; the transformation that had taken place in my spirit had yet to flow into my soul.

For many years, I sought this mysterious healing of the soul but settled for an assurance that someday I would feel whole again. About 14 years later, Roland Kurth, who headed up Campus Crusade Switzerland, came to Access and taught a three-day seminar on inner healing and deliverance. In his teaching, I found the path to bring my mind, will, and emotions into the same transformation I experienced in my spirit. Roland called it inner healing.

The seminar material was from a book by Dr. Charles Kraft called *Defeating Dark Angels*, and it set the foundation for inner healing and deliverance. Roland distinguished between these two, saying that inner healing is a process of exchanging lies embedded in our value system for the truth of God's Word, whereas deliverance is being set free from demonic influence.

TWO KINGDOMS IN CONFLICT

The Scripture speaks of two kingdoms in conflict: the Kingdom of God versus the kingdom of darkness. In Ephesians, Paul draws a clear picture of the conflict:

> *For we are not fighting against flesh-and-blood enemies, but against evil rulers and authorities of the unseen world, against mighty powers in this dark world, and against evil spirits in the heavenly places. — Ephesians 6:12*

Here is another key: the transformation that God is working in us takes place on a battlefield. The inner room where moments of decision take place is a battleground, and we have an enemy who will do anything to defeat us and keep us from reflecting God's glory. His strategy is to keep us oblivious to the things God has prepared for us and occupy us with urgent but not important things.

According to the Bible, Satan was the highest form of all of God's creation, but he rebelled;[64] consequently, he was cast out from God's presence to Earth, where he was given dominion for a set time. Filled with pride, hate, and envy, Satan retaliated against God by pulling humans down with him. When sin entered the world through Adam's act of rebellion against God, it corrupted all creation and impaired its ability to worship God. Because of sin, God cast humankind out of His presence, placing us under Satan's dominion, along with all the rebel demons. The

---

[64] Isaiah 14:12–15.

intimate fellowship we once enjoyed with God broke and our freedom to choose came under the oppressive influence of Satan and his kingdom of darkness. Satan holds a legal right to rule over us because of our sin, and the sentence of death bound us to him with chains.

This captivity is the state of the world without Jesus Christ, separated from God and hostile toward Him. But when Jesus Christ took on flesh and became a man, He did not have a sinful nature; He was not subject to sin or death or Satan. Yet He chose to take upon Himself our sin; the death sentence we earned, He paid on the cross. He carried our sin, our shame, and our death sentence as well. On the third day, Jesus rose from the dead. He conquered death, broke the chains that bound humanity to Satan, and set us free from the dominion of Satan and his kingdom. And on the cross, Jesus clothed us in His righteousness, made us holy, and gave us eternal life.[65]

The death and resurrection of Jesus Christ is the most significant moment in all time; in it, He redeemed, reconciled, and restored all that was broken or lost in the fall of humankind. The cross has legal ramifications, as well as moral, emotional, intellectual, and spiritual impact. It affects every corner of human awareness and reality. On the cross, the Kingdom of God defeated the kingdom of darkness.

When we engage in the battle of the two kingdoms, our role is to walk in victory in the footsteps of Jesus, who has conquered Satan and set us free. Without any further claim over us, Satan still has two strategies left to employ against us: to accuse and deceive. Satan can speak to people's sinful nature, and through it, he can plant thoughts in our minds. Amazingly, he manages to maintain a presence in the inner room of our hearts at the moment of decision. His plan for those who believe in Jesus Christ is to isolate them, distract them from the battle, and talk them into laying down their weapons against him. It is so sad to consider that this describes the majority of our congregations in the US: we are isolated, distracted, disarmed, neutralized Christians.

---

[65] Remember the Holiness–Righteousness Cycle?

LIES AND ACCUSATIONS

Our webs of transforming relationships are particularly threatening to Satan, so he is doing all he can to destroy these with accusations and deception. He moves to break our relationship with God by slandering Him with false accusations of pride and selfishness. Satan's strategies are the reason Jesus calls him a liar and the father of lies[66] and the accuser of the brethren.[67] Satan's lies and accusations are targeted against God, others, and ourselves. He makes his case before the throne of God when he can, and in the minds of believers frequently, using every opportunity to twist the truth and hand us a faux brick with which to build our lives. Satan begins this process very early in our lives, even as newborn infants.[68] In time, the lies about God, others, and self that Satan hands us become part of our belief system, locked away deep within our psyche, in the hollows of our soul. Like mutant genes on a chromosome or a bug in a software program, they hide unnoticed while they wreak havoc on our bodies, causing disease and despair.

The lies and accusations' effect is often dormant, lurking in the background, but they are the root of addiction, anger, and wickedness. They can become strongholds of sin, even for believers.

STRONGHOLDS OF SIN

A stronghold of sin is a place in the believer's heart where he or she does not submit to the Holy Spirit. It happens at the moment of decision; despite the Holy Spirit's prompting, we repeatedly choose to rebel against God. I have suffered from strongholds, and other saints who are very near and dear to me have experienced suffering as well. In every case, the result has been the destruction of relationships. The effect of these strongholds is to isolate the believer from God and His household. Once separated, the believer becomes distracted from the spiritual battle and lays down the armor of God. Some spend their entire lives in this state, waiting to be set free through the gospel of Jesus Christ.

---

[66] John 8:44.
[67] Revelation 12:10.
[68] I described this process in more detail in the section on the FDD.

Living in sin is the exact antithesis of being transformed by the gospel of Jesus Christ. Transformation happens in the presence of God, and sin kicks us out of His presence; it prevents transformation. Strongholds of sin are a major reason many believers in Jesus Christ are not experiencing the gospel's transforming power in their lives.

Sin isolates the believer from God and His household. In John 3:20–21, Jesus shares this insight with Nicodemus: "All who do evil hate the light and refuse to go near it for fear their sins will be exposed. But those who do what is right come to light so others can see that they are doing what God wants." Relationships break for many reasons, and sin is one of them. To walk in victory on the battlefield, the believer must remove the hindrance of sin.

INNER HEALING

Inner healing is a process of restoration of the soul mediated by the Holy Spirit in believers' lives. The process can be simulated in unbelievers as well, but in that case, it is not built on the solid foundation of the Word of God and not mediated by the Holy Spirit. Therefore, in unbelievers, inner healing is prone to be only temporary and partial relief, not true redemption. But for believers, it brings freedom from strongholds of sin.

One useful tool that we have used is inner healing sessions. It's where members of a web of transforming relationships intentionally seek God, asking Him to heal one of its members. This meeting is neither counseling nor psychological analysis. The session's goal is to wait on the Holy Spirit to reveal one specific lie planted in the seeker's beliefs and replace it with the truth of God's Word. The truth will then set the seeker free from the strongholds of sin that the lie caused. A seeker can go through periodic sessions as often as needed.

A large group from many churches in Lebanon attended Roland Kurth's seminar on inner healing and deliverance. Although we had no previous experience, the seminar gave us a reputation among other churches as people who could do inner healing and cast out demons. Consequently, many people called our team to schedule healing sessions.

A healing session consists of the person who needs healing, whom I call the seeker, and a team, the listeners, sitting around a table. Listeners pray for the seeker over several days before the appointed time. The session begins with the seeker telling about a stronghold they have struggled with but have been unable to uproot independently. The listeners then wait on God to reveal one specific incident, usually a trauma, in the person's past and ask them to talk about it. The Spirit of God often reveals something either directly to the seeker or in words and images of insight to one or more listeners. If there is no revelation, then it is not God's timing for healing, and the session should be postponed.

The stage of waiting on God requires a great deal of discipline by the listeners not to project their opinions or thoughts on what the Holy Spirit says. While the seeker tells their story, the listeners may start to form an idea about the probable cause, but this idea is not what I mean by a word from the Holy Spirit. The listeners must have enough experience to distinguish God's voice from their own and resist the urge to advise the seeker.

The listeners then write the word they received, if any, and hand it to a moderator. The moderator then presents these words to the seeker to see if they mean anything to them, and they often do. We have seen so many people look at a drawing or listen to some words that seemed meaningless to everyone else, only to break down in tears. This reminder brings an event or trauma they suffered to mind, and they share it with the group. The event was usually when they embraced a lie that developed into a stronghold in their lives.

Once we have identified the trauma the Holy Spirit wants to address, we then ask the seeker to tell the story of the incident and recount how he or she felt. It usually includes some abusive or hurtful actions that led the seeker to swallow a lie from the devil.

For example, one seeker recollected, "The last time I saw my mother was in a park, and I can still see her walking away. That was when I realized I was a liability and that I was not worthy of love." He faced the trauma of his mother leaving, and he had to explain why, so he inferred from it a lie about himself and God that became implanted in his self-image: "I am not worthy of God's love." At that point in the session, the seeker was in tears. We then asked him to pray and ask Jesus where He was when his mother left him, to ask Jesus what He felt when this happened. We then proceeded to help the seeker find the truth about these questions in the Word of God in verses that directly contradict the lie he or she received. For the seeker who thought he was unworthy of love, God gave us Psalm 139.

You made all the delicate, inner parts of my body and knit me together in my mother's womb.

Thank you for making me so wonderfully complex! Your workmanship is marvelous—how well I know it.

You watched me as I was being formed in utter seclusion, as I was woven together in the dark of the womb.

You saw me before I was born.
Every day of my life was recorded in your book.

Every moment was laid out before a single day had passed.

How precious are your thoughts about me, O God. They cannot be numbered!

I can't even count them;
they outnumber the grains of sand!

And when I wake up,
you are still with me!

—Psalm 139:13–18

We had some astounding results from inner healing sessions. On many occasions, the Holy Spirit guided us in prayer, visions, and dreams to recall specific traumatic events, then led us to identify the malignant lies that spread disease in believers' lives. We were then able to clean them out and destroy them with the truth of the Bible. John 8:32 is a word from Jesus to His disciples: "And you will know the truth, and the truth will set you free." In his seminar, Roland described the process as Jesus opening the door to the basement in our heart, walking down the steps, and finding the lie filed away in the deep recesses. He would then remove it and replace it with truth from the Word of God. That was an excellent illustration of inner healing and an image that has stuck with me over the years.

DELIVERANCE

As if it is not enough that strongholds of sin leave us devastated and unable to experience the transformation God intended for us, they can also lead to demonic oppression. Some ask, "Is it possible for a believer to come under demonic oppression? After all, when we became believers in Jesus Christ, we became His possession, and the Holy Spirit came to live in us. How can demons and the Holy Spirit both live in the same person?" The answer is that no demon can possess a believer in Jesus Christ, but they can influence him or her to the point of oppression. There is a difference between possession and oppression, like the difference between owning a home and renting one. The rental contract does not convey ownership of the property but only its use. In the case of believers under demonic oppression, they have somehow conveyed a right to demons, permitting them to use their bodies and influence their minds, will, and emotions.

The *continuous* presence of sin in our lives can lead to demonic oppression. Emphasis on the word "continuous" distinguishes between isolated sinful acts and a lifestyle of sin. A famous quote attributed to Martin Luther says, "You cannot keep birds from flying over your head, but you can keep them from building a nest in your hair." In other words, it is one thing to have a sinful thought and then cast it out of your mind, and it is another to allow it to grow into a habit that traps you in a lifestyle of sin.

A missionary couple visited us at Access one day. Their visit coincided with a deliverance session we were having for a friend, who was not a believer but came asking for deliverance from demons. He said he went to visit someone in the Beqaa valley who claimed that he was a medium for evil spirits. Our friend challenged the medium, saying he thought it was all nonsense. The medium opened a book and read portions from it, then waved his hand over the page as if to scoop the air over it and hurled it toward our friend. He did this several times, and the friend said it was like something punched him in the chest every time he did. For the next two months, he was miserable, depressed, and fearful. The missionary couple listened to the story and then asked me if they could show us how they learned to deal with demons. I agreed, so they proceeded to ask the Holy Spirit to reveal to us if there were demons involved and, if so, to tell us their names so we could cast them out.

There was silence for about two or three minutes. Then the missionary said, "Spirit of violence, in the name of Jesus Christ, I command you to leave." My friend exhaled. Then a minute later, the missionary said, "Spirit of despair, I command you to leave." Again my friend exhaled. Then the missionary spoke a third time, saying, "Spirit of murder, get out." And for the third time, my relative sighed heavily and collapsed. We revived him with some water and shared the good news of the death, burial, and resurrection of Jesus Christ. With tears and repentance, he prayed to receive Jesus. Ever since the missionary couple showed us how to wait on the Holy Spirit, we have used this method to cast out demons. There is no need to address the demons or pick a fight with them—just cast them out like roaches. It's house cleaning made easy.

So, we have learned several things about deliverance; demons are like roaches, infestations of filth that must be cleaned. Deliverance should not become a focus of the believer's walk with Jesus. It is like pest control or housekeeping, something we have to do to stay healthy, but it is not our main occupation. Making disciples of all nations has to remain our focus.

Defeating Dark Angels by Charles Kraft showed me the critical connection between spiritual warfare and sin. He described sin as garbage and demons as rodents. The filth of garbage attracts mice, and in the same way, sin attracts demons to a person's life. Kraft teaches that if you want to get rid of demons, get rid of the pile of sin in your life. Then, once the demons are gone, there is no more garbage to attract them back.

Inner healing and deliverance from demonic oppression are valuable tools that Jesus has made available to us. They can help many overcome addictions and other stubborn habits that keep us from walking in victory and experiencing the transformation He desires for us.

CONCLUSION

This book has outlined the biblical foundations of transforming relationships and has given a detailed description of what they are. It is time to tie things together in an action plan.

Three main thoughts to keep in mind are first that transformation is a state of relatedness to God in which the believer enters His presence, sees Him, and reflects His glory.

Second, to be related to God is to be a member of His household. Relationships with God and others are the context in which we experience and reflect God. We walk with God not as individuals but as communities.

Third, your love affair with God is a unique story, and you are authoring it together with Him. It is not a generic one-size-fits-all formula but an individual act of creation by God. Your transformation is one of a kind, not a cookie-cutter production line, which means that the action plan to reach your individual goal has been tailor-made for you. There is no need to fret about finding your plan because the Holy Spirit is in charge of that task, and "He who began a good work in you will complete it" (Philippians 1:6). The action plan for transformation will help you inhabit the powerful, customized life of discipleship that the Holy Spirit has prepared for you.

AN ACTION PLAN FOR TRANSFORMATION

I hope that you are asking yourself, "How do I get into a transforming relationship?" Transforming relationships, after all, are the building blocks of transforming communities.

Through this book, I have tried to explain the need for transforming relationships; the companion book *Transforming Communities* will make a case for pursuing the same kind of transformation as a larger community. But desiring transformation is merely the first step. I have prepared a separate resource to serve as a practical guide for you and your team as you pursue this goal. It is called the Transformation Series Online. It covers three domains of transformation that run concurrently. The first focuses on forming the transforming relationships illustrated in this book, and it addresses believers individually. The second describes how to build a transforming team, as shown in *Transforming Community*, and addresses the group as a community. The third is a dialogue among transforming teams as we seek to discern the times.

Here is an outline of the first domain, which is how to build a transforming relationship:

1. Leave and Cleave. It's your decision whether to believe in Jesus Christ or not. Do you believe that Jesus Christ is God, that He came and dwelt among us, died for our sins, and rose from the dead? If you reflect on these questions and sense that your heart is saying yes, confirm your faith by praying to ask Jesus to enter your life. Also, leave your old spiritual family. Before you can cleave to the household of God, you must leave Satan's dominion; you are no longer under his authority!

2. Form or join a group of believers. Start by connecting with at least one other person who wants to walk with Jesus Christ. Agree to build a transforming relationship, as outlined in chapter 7 of this book. Pray together and ask God to guide you as you seek to determine your calling, both individually and collectively. Unity with Christ and the other members of the team is the goal. With Jesus at the center of the relationship, serve, submit, learn how to resolve conflicts, and accept one another.

3. Learn to study, meditate on, and understand the Bible. One obstacle that prevents believers from hearing the voice of the Holy Spirit is that we have deferred the study and interpretation of the Word of God to experts. Seminaries are graduating teachers who reiterate their prescribed theological discourse. Members of congregations eat up the canned product, and it becomes their standard spiritual food. It is time to get off canned spiritual food and start preparing

your own with a fresh word from God every day. Believers in a transforming relationship must know the difference between an observation and an interpretation of the Word of God.

4. Learn to listen to the Holy Spirit. A relationship with God is only as good as your ability to hear His voice. Communicating with God goes hand in hand with meditating on the Word of God. As we seek His presence in the Word of God with a prayerful heart, His Spirit speaks to us. Many churches discourage this practice because they are concerned that people will come up with strange ideas and declare, "This is what God has said." This threat is why we need each other to affirm or correct us when we wrongly believe a word is from the Lord.

5. Come into the presence of God daily as individuals and as a team. Worship is at the core of transformation. Get a notebook and write down verses that reveal something about God. Make a list of all the verses you accumulate over weeks or months and use it to worship Him[69]. Repeat back to Him what you see in His Word. Do this alone and with your team as often as you can. Put your prayers together in song and sing it out loud to the Lord. If you prefer, do the same using paint, poetry, dance, or whatever else is meaningful to you. I have enjoyed using gardening as a way to express my love and worship to God.

6. Discern your calling as an individual. Meditate on verses that command you to do something. For instance, "Be holy" (1 Peter 1:15), "Give thanks" (Ephesians 5:20), "Love one another" (1 John 4:7), "Do not lie" (Exodus 20:16), "Do not steal" (Exodus 20:15), "Do not commit adultery" (Exodus 20:14), and "Bear one another's burdens" (Galatians 6:2). Make a list of these commands; this is your general calling. Next, ask God for discernment and write out what you believe God created you for (Ephesians 2:10). Review your culture and the significant events that have shaped

---

[69] Transforming Community has published an app called Worship. You can download it from the App Store or Google Play. You can also go to www.transformingcommunity.com to sign up for the newsletter and get a link to download the app.

you.[70] These are indicators of God's unique calling on your life. Do this with your team as well and ask for their perspective.

7. Discern your calling as a team. As teammates, study one another. Understand how God shapes each member because this will help you understand why He brought you together as a team.

8. Remove strongholds in your team and your community with inner healing and deliverance. Start exercising spiritual power as a team and destroy every stronghold or root of bitterness that prevents you and those around you from experiencing intimacy with God.

If you are ready to take the next step in your transformation journey, join Transforming Community Online for guided instruction. You can sign up at www.transformingcommunity.com.

A WORD FOR THE CHURCH IN AMERICA

On May 26, 2020, riots broke out in cities across the United States. They started as a protest against the brutal killing of George Floyd by a police officer during an arrest in Minneapolis, Minnesota. The riots that followed were an eruption of anger pent up in people of all backgrounds, providing those who want to destroy America with an opportunity to advance their goals. These are symptoms of the grave problem of ethnocentricity that I wrote about in chapter 3, and it is tearing our country apart.

God has shaken us to the core and showed us that America needs healing! The kind of healing that only Jesus can perform. But where is the church? Why are we so helpless to bring healing? Sermons by Christian leaders seek to raise awareness and passion, yet there has been little response. It seems all we can do is talk.

We cannot give what we don't have. How can we ask America to be transformed if we have not changed? We have many words and theories, but so far, our deeds merely emulate the world. We are busy vying for the biggest congregation, the most massive budget, and the best programs. We are in love with our organizations, and we run them the way we learned

---

[70] Clinton, J. Robert. The Making of a Leader: Recognizing the Lessons and Stages of Leadership Development. Colorado Springs, CO: NavPress, 1988.

it in management schools. Unfortunately, the church in America marches lock-step with the world's system; how can it lead?

Jesus said that in the last days, the Kingdom of Heaven would be like ten virgins who took their lamps and went out to meet the bridegroom.[71] Some brought along oil for their lamps, while others didn't. Today, the church in America is like one of the virgins whose lamp has run out of oil. Instead of shining our light on our Savior, we are busy with internal issues and preparation for the work we ought to be doing.

In the parable, the foolish virgins took too long fetching oil and missed the bridegroom's arrival. But it is not too late for us. We can change. We can connect in transforming relationships that will transform our communities, our country, and the world.

The Church can move mountains when it enters into the presence of God to worship! We don't need more money or better organizations. We don't even need more analysis and information. What we do need is to worship God. Will you enter His presence now and worship Him?

One resource to help you worship God is an app called The Worship App. It is available for free at the App Store and the Google Play Store. Search for Worship App by Transforming Community and download it today. It provides an extensive list of Bible verses that reveal something about God. They are organized in sixty-seven categories under three headings, His Essence, His Names, and His Attributes. You can begin by meditating on a verse and praying audibly to God what it says about Him. You can also share your reflections with friends on the App.

A WORD FOR THE PEOPLE OF THE MIDDLE EAST

In the last two decades, most Middle East nations have regressed to the dark ages while the rest of the world advances. Our people are among the least productive and most oppressed on Earth. Literacy in Lebanon has reverted to what it used to be before World War II. Syria has been drowning in a bloodbath for the past eight years and lies in ruins. With its ideological and financial ties to Iran, Hizbollah has conscripted Lebanese

---

[71] Matthew 25:1–13

lives, families, and resources to its cause. They have fostered governments that are a den of thieves. These crooked Lebanese politicians have given Hizbollah constitutional legitimacy, in exchange of shielding them from prosecution for stealing the nation's wealth. Even the judicial system has become entangled in this malignancy. The Middle East needs deliverance!

God has allowed these disasters to pour out on us for a reason. He wants to bring us to our knees and to persuade us to let go of our pride and come to Him. Our earthly leaders have betrayed us, and they have stolen our children's future. Turn to Jesus! He will not betray us.

We must let go of the hatred that fills our souls and sets us in conflict with everyone around us. We must abandon bloodshed and violence and enter the peace of Jesus Christ. He is our only hope.

APPENDIX

The group's influence in our private moments of decision makes it imperative to understand how it exerts its effect. How do people decide to buy one product over another? What would cause a person to choose to commit a terrorist act, killing innocent people? Classical thinking focuses on a person's character, which is partly involved, but that does not provide a full picture.

The 9/11 attacks in 2001 exposed the existence of a network of terrorists called Al Qaeda. As they entered into the spotlight, the need to conquer them became a global demand. This demand resulted in new studies aimed at understanding their structure and how they produced people willing to kill themselves and others. That led to a more in-depth investigation of group dynamics and, more specifically, Complexity Theory (or CT).

Complexity is a relatively recent theory that came out of organizational management, and it offers an alternative to the traditional scientific method. In the traditional method, experimental analysis breaks down a complicated system into its smallest observable components, develops an understanding of its attributes and interactions, and draws conclusions based on these components' sum effect. The findings of an analytical study are predictable and precise within a specified degree of variation. This method is called the analytical– deconstructive approach. Complexity is different; it is neither analytical nor deconstructive. It is experiential, which means that it does not produce a model that approximates the process under study but is a picture of the actual procedure. What you see is what it is; in that sense, it is less abstract than the analytical–deconstructive approach.

Complexity Theory is useful for understanding systems that exist in nature yet do not conform or behave according to a consistent set of laws with reproducible results. These systems have a high degree of chaos, out of which new cohesive systems may emerge.[72]

An example of a complex system is a forest; it has grass, plants, shrubs, trees, soil, rocks, rivers, animals, insects, fungi, and many other organisms. It attracts life because it provides shelter from weather and predators, food for a wide variety of organisms, and beauty and serenity. The forest behaves and operates at a level beyond any of its parts. A blade of grass in the forest produces chlorophyll, converting sunlight to food energy that eventually passes on to an animal. Many blades of grass in the front lawn of a house operate in the same way, but the effect is different: they produce a beautiful landscape that makes a home more desirable and worth more money. The blade of grass didn't behave differently from one case to another, but how it related to other elements around it led to the emergence of a different outcome. Four key concepts in CT are worth mentioning to appreciate its suitability to understand church and family dynamics. First is the idea of emergence. Emergence refers to a phenomenon that arises from elements connected in a configuration that results in a system-level behavior. Depending on the number of elements in a system, they can be combined or configured in many different ways. The way they are connected determines the system-level behavior that emerges. Various configurations can lead to different results, and not all of them lead to viable or sustainable emergent systems; most lead to chaos. Emergence is a significant point of CT. Some scholars view it as a running experiment that continues to fail and disintegrate into chaos, then reiterates with a new configuration of the elements until a new system emerges. Several systems relate in different configurations until a higher level arises—a network of systems. Then these networks relate, and so on.

The second is non-linearity. Most systems observed in nature behave in counter-intuitive ways; instead of moving toward equilibrium or neutrality, they seem to favor a fall from the equilibrium state. Non-linearity is true

---

[72] The word "emerge" may bring to mind related terms such as "emerging," "emergent," and "emergence," which describe recent movements of the church in the US. It may be that some of the terminology used to describe that movement came from CT literature. Unfortunately, the use of the word "emerge" or any variation thereof may imply agreement with whatever doctrine or strategy those churches advance. In this instance, I am using the term as it relates to CT only, without reference to the Emergent Church movement in the US.

of many systems, including human social interaction. In a non-linear system, group behavior cannot be defined or calculated as the sum of all its members' actions. The two are qualitatively different, like apples and oranges. Human culture is one example of a non-linear system; it cannot be defined by individuals' behavior but only as a group.

The third key concept is called adaptive behavior. Elements in a system respond to outward pressures with reactions that allow the whole group to adapt to change; they learn and modify their behavior to favor the desired outcome. Hence, the adaptive system gradually closes in on a cohesive solution that allows the system to persist or causes a new one to emerge. These are called Complex Adaptive Systems.

Fourth is network theory. Complex systems can be visualized well as a network of elements connected by relationships. The network's total sum output can come to be defined by the links that connect the components.

Complexity Theory seems difficult to understand initially, but it is a complicated speech that describes familiar concepts. In CT, the study focuses on the emergence of new systems from the adaptive behavior of elements in an existing system. What some missiologists call "movement" is called "system" in CT; in other words, it focuses on how transformation spreads through a group of people.

I wanted to take the time to explain CT because it communicates well what we experienced as a church-planting team in Lebanon. A critical component of the theory that I find useful is that it helps us observe people in relationships and identify the forces that guide them to live as disciples of Jesus Christ.

The classic example given in CT is that of a flock of birds swarming in the sky. How do they all know when to turn left or right? Is there one leader who appoints small group leaders, who each disseminate commands on cue? Not at all; studies have found that there is no leadership hierarchy in flocks of birds, yet there is "something" leading them. As each bird (CT calls them elements in a system) reacts to the context in which it is flying, it adjusts its flying trajectory to a simple set of rules that each bird in the flock can follow. Each bird understands that it must not bump into the bird next to it and that it must stay together with its fellows, so it does not become vulnerable to predation. The obedience of each bird to the guidelines, which CT calls an "adaptive behavior," emerges as a group or system-level behavior that is not determined or predicted by elements in the system. Technically, in birds' flight patterns, the whole flock's direction comes from how the birds relate to each other. Did you notice what I just said? The flock administration comes from the way they connect, not from a hierarchy of leading birds.

Complexity Theory is useful in studying the different dynamics of transformation and precisely how they impact the moment of decision. The take-home message for the family of God—itself a complex system—is that relationships have influence. Traditional studies of group behavior may focus solely on the group participants' individual characteristics, but in this case, the focus is on the relationships between them. The way we are connected matters more than personal gifting or abilities. It is not only a question of whether we connect to the people of God but how we are connected; the answer will impact our decisions and, ultimately, our transformation. Keep this in mind as we progress in our study of transformation.

BIBLIOGRAPHY

Amer, Muhammad, Tugrul U. Daim, and Antonie Jetter. A Review of Scenario Planning. *Futures* 46: 23–40, 2013.

Barna, George. New Marriage and Divorce Statistics Released. *Barna Group,* March 31, 2008.

Covey, Stephen R. *The Seven Habits of Highly Effective People: Powerful Lessons in Personal Change.* New York, NY: Simon and Schuster, 1989.

Ferguson, David, Teresa Ferguson, Terri Ferguson, and Carole Gift Page. *Intimate Encounters: A Practical Guide to Discovering the Secrets of a Really Great Marriage.* Austin, TX: Intimacy Press, 1997.

Graham, Will. "10 Differences Between Luther and Zwingli: How to Differentiate Between the Two Protestant Reformers?" *Evangelical Focus.* August 3, 2019.

Henrichson, Walter. "Many Aspire, Few Attain." Colorado Springs: NavPress Publishing Group, 2008.

Kifner, John. "Armenian Genocide of 1915: An Overview" NY: New York Times archive, n.d.

Kraft, Charles H. *Defeating Dark Angels: Breaking Demonic Oppression in the Believer's Life.* Ventura, CA: Regal Books, 1992.

Mason, Mike. *The Mystery of Marriage, 20th Anniversary Edition.* Colorado Springs, CO: Multnomah Press, 2005.

Newbigin, Lesslie. *The Household of God: Lectures on the Nature of the Church.* Eugene, OR: Wiph and Stock, 2008.

Piper, John. *Let the Nations Be Glad!: The Supremacy of God in Missions.* Grand Rapids, MI: Baker Books, 1993.

Walls, Andrew F. *The Cross-Cultural Process in Christian History: Studies in the Transmission and Appropriation of Faith.* Maryknoll, NY: Orbis Books, 2002.

Wasserman, Stanley and Katherine Faust. *Social Network Analysis: Methods and Applications.* Cambridge; NY: Cambridge University Press, 1994.

Zylstra, Sarah Eekhoff. Why Pastors Are Committing Suicide. *TheGospelCoalition.org, November 23, 2016.*

Lightning Source UK Ltd.
Milton Keynes UK
UKHW041858080421
381687UK00007B/426/J